AMERICAN ILLUSTRATION
1890—1925
ROMANCE, ADVENTURE & SUSPENSE

AMERICAN ILLUSTRATION
1890—1925
ROMANCE, ADVENTURE & SUSPENSE

JUDY L. LARSON
GLENBOW MUSEUM • CALGARY, ALBERTA, CANADA

AMERICAN ILLUSTRATION 1890—1925
ROMANCE, ADVENTURE AND SUSPENSE

This volume has been produced by the
GLENBOW MUSEUM, CALGARY
with the assistance of the
CANADA COUNCIL,
PROVINCE OF ALBERTA and
CITY OF CALGARY.

©Glenbow-Alberta Institute, 1986
All rights reserved.
Printed in Canada.
ISBN 0-919224-47-4
Glenbow Museum
130—9th Avenue S.E.
Calgary, Alberta
Canada, T2G 0P3

Front Cover:
Norman Mills Price
Detail of cover design
for *St. Nicholas Magazine*,
September, 1916
Cat. no. 118

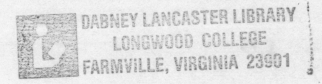

CONTENTS

Foreword 7

Acknowledgements 9

Tribute to Helen Card 11

Introduction 19

The Periodicals 39

The Books 47

The Illustrations 51

The Smart Set 59

The Masses 63

The Domestic Scene 69

Town and Country 75

Let Me Call You Sweetheart 79

Deeds of Derring Do 85

Mystery and Suspense 91

The Great Outdoors 95

Dream Days 99

War! 105

The Sporting Life 111

Faraway Places 115

Epilogue 119

Biographies 123

Bibliography 149

Catalogue of the Exhibition 151

Itinerary of the Exhibition 159

FOREWORD

It has often been said that the collections of the Glenbow-Alberta Institute in Calgary, Canada, contain many surprises some of which are yet to be discovered. It is certainly true that the collections are vast and span several disciplines and that the backlog of documentation, cataloguing and research, though a function of its short but exciting history, is nonetheless substantial.

The presence of a collection of more than five thousand works by American illustrators in a Canadian collection is one of those surprises.

To provide a context it should be explained that the Glenbow-Alberta Institute, better known as the Glenbow Museum, is among other things a very important archives of photographs and manuscripts related to the history of western Canada and a large research library with the same focus, and also a museum of ethnology with strengths in the indigenous peoples of Canada, particularly the West, but also international collections from Africa, Central and South America, Australia, and Indonesia. Then there is the museum of cultural history which like the library and archives, is concerned with western Canada, and the art museum with strengths in western Canadian historical painting as well as Canadian modern and contemporary work. There is also the museum of military history which holds, in addition to the collections related to the Canadian military in Colonial and post-Confederation periods, both Japanese and European armour and an important collection of military and non-military firearms and edge weapons of the last five centuries. There is also a significant international collection of minerals and an outstanding collection of Canadian coins and currency.

If you add to all of the above the expected support services and technical facilities you have the Institute, surprises and all. The history of Glenbow is relatively short. It goes back only to 1955 when the late Eric L. Harvie created the Glenbow Foundation. In 1966 the Foundation's assets were transferred to the Province of Alberta and the Glenbow-Alberta Institute was created as a public institution. The Institute today is one of the half dozen or so major custodial institutions in Canada and the largest of these west of the Province of Ontario.

During the early years of the Glenbow Foundation and later the Institute, the Harvie family and other benefactors were laying the foundation for a major museum in the West. They collected during a time when the amassing of significant holdings was much more feasible than it is today and the Glenbow collections, with all their diversity, could not realistically be recreated in the last two decades of this century.

It is interesting to know that the collection of American illustration began in 1956 when the Glenbow Foundation was acquiring works from the Latendorf Book Shop in New York City. That collecting continued with the help of Walter Latendorf and later with the support of Helen Card who succeeded him as the bookshop's owner. And then in 1969, the Riveredge Foundation which had also been created by Mr. Harvie, acquired the bulk of the present holding from Helen Card shortly before her death. This last purchase was for more than forty-five hundred drawings and paintings by more than seven hundred and fifty illustrators spanning the period from 1850 to 1950, but with an emphasis on the "Golden Age" of American illustration, 1890 to 1930.

The collections of the Riveredge Foundation came into Glenbow's possession in 1979 and the total holdings are only now being studied and presented to the public in exhibitions and publications such as this.

It should be mentioned that the first exhibition derived from the collection was the work of Charles Livingston Bull, presented in 1979 and curated by Peter White, then an Assistant Curator in the Art Department at Glenbow, who also authored the accompanying catalogue. The present exhibition is the first attempt to draw from the entire collection and to explore both its scope and depth. Beyond doubt there will be many future exhibitions as further research indicates new ways of examining the work of American illustrators who thus far seem to have attracted the interest of art historians and curators only spasmodically over the years.

The Glenbow Museum feels privileged to hold this important collection both as a means to publication and exhibition and as a research resource for scholars in the field. We are also honoured to have Judy Larson as a guest curator at this time and hope that she and others will work with us in the future on ever more intelligent insights into this fascinating chapter of art in America.

Duncan F. Cameron, Director

ACKNOWLEDGEMENTS

n 1975 my graduate advisor Dr. E. Maurice Bloch mentioned Helen Card and her collection of drawings for American book and periodical illustration, but it was not until 1981 that I located the collection at the Glenbow Museum and made the acquaintance of Peter White, then Assistant Curator of Art. It was through Mr. White's encouragement that I came to Calgary as a consultant to help organize and identify drawings in the collection. Excited by the range and quality of drawings in that collection, I have returned to the Glenbow to organize this exhibition *American Illustration 1890-1925: Romance, Adventure and Suspense.*

The staff of the Glenbow has been excellent in arranging details, organizing schedules, and keeping the whole project co-ordinated and moving smoothly. Duncan Cameron, Director, was helpful in his support of the project from its beginning. Barbara Tyler helped secure funding for the exhibition. Rick Budd co-ordinated the production of the catalogue which was designed by Cathie Faren and typeset by Luana Russell. Ruth Bertelsen Fraser edited the manuscript. Colleen O'Neill and Christopher Jackson proofread the manuscript. Maeve Spain assisted with the cataloguing and the photography. Kevin Oke was the photographer for the catalogue. Unfortunately the drawings for illustrations were in a bad state of conservation because of their ephemeral materials and circumstances. Ann Gardner worked on the conservation of the drawings and Ewa Smithwick worked on the conservation of the paintings, rendering them suitable for the exhibition. The works were matted by Gordon Duggan, Patricia Olynyk and Tawny Kohut, and framed by Terry Hagen. But especially, my thanks go to Patricia Ainslie, Assistant Curator of Art at the Glenbow Museum, who assisted me in so many ways and made the distance between Atlanta, Georgia, and Calgary, Alberta seen manageable. She established both the tour and organized the production of the catalogue.

Many institutions were helpful in my research. I would like to specifically thank Ann Brown at the Brandywine River Museum and Terry Brown at the Society of Illustrators. Also, I wish to thank the staffs of the Delaware Art Museum, New York Public Library, Pennsylvania Historical Society, Library of Congress, Boston Public Library, Cincinnati Art Museum, Proctor and Gamble Company, American Antiquarian Society, and the Worcester Public Library.

Lastly, my special thanks to Phyllis Peet, Beverly Larson, and Steven Otfinoski who read the manuscript and offered valuable contributions.

Judy L. Larson, Guest Curator

TRIBUTE TO HELEN CARD

oremost among the collectors and dealers who preserved and promoted illustrator art as a legitimate art form was Helen Card, of The Latendorf Bookshop in New York. The following tribute was prepared by Maurice Bloch, former Director of Grunwald Center for the Graphic Arts and Professor Emeritus, UCLA, Los Angeles, California.

Helen Card, Springfield, Vermont, 1956
Photograph courtesy of Maurice Bloch

11

espite the lapse of many years, I still retain a distinct memory of Helen "Teri" Card, the tall, handsome, dark-haired, vivacious woman whose open manner and crisp, witty conversation easily set her apart from almost everyone I came into contact with in those days. I recall meeting her in New York early in 1951 during one of my periodic visits to the Mannados Bookshop in mid-town Manhattan. The shop had become a meeting place of sorts for bibliophiles and collectors of material relating to the American West, as well as for the few enthusiasts who wanted to see original work by artist-illustrators and share information about that neglected area of art history in this country.

Because a sharp distinction had long existed between the so-called "fine artist," who ostensibly creates his own visions and ideas, and the artist whose work necessarily complements expression in another medium not of his making, the stigma attached to illustration left an indelible mark upon the field, and in particular upon the men and women associated with it professionally. With the possible exception of scholars life Frank Weitenkampf and Theodore Bolton, who attempted to keep their names and reputations alive, illustrators were almost all forgotten and their works consistently excluded from most public collections. The sharp dichotomy of value judgments, that so often involved a single personality, only served to spark my curiosity and deepening interest, and I spent all my spare time searching old books and magazines in an effort to acquaint myself with their work. Since both E. Walter Latendorf, the proprietor of Mannados, and Teri Card, had made their personal discoveries in the 1930s, I surmise that their close friendship must have developed to a large extent through their mutual involvement with illustration.

In any event, any impressions I can now evoke of Teri Card and her times must inevitably lead to a characterization of Walter Latendorf, an unforgettable personality who became a bookman after a career as personal manager of Singer's Midgets, a travelling circus troupe that enjoyed an international reputation in its day. As a dealer in books, he was still a showman who enjoyed nothing more than to play host to a circle of close friends who gathered weekly at the bookshop to quench their thirst for spirits and good conversation. Once the guests arrived, generally about three in the afternoon, they were expected to take their places around a large circular dining-room table Latendorf set up for that purpose in the lower level of his shop. All seemed to know instinctively where to sit since liquid refreshment selected to satisfy individual taste was always located beneath the table close to each chair. Some regulars, such as Mahonri Young, the veteran painter and sculptor, were occassionally joined by out-of-town visitors. Once the "knights of the round table" had become sufficiently mellowed by several hours of good cheer, the host took everyone to dinner at a nearby restaurant, where more toasting ensued. These events were for "men only," although Teri recalled similar experiences when she dedicated her Howard Pyle catalogue to "the man who was always to be found in the old Mannados Bookshop, with its conversational lunches, its hospitality, its gay Wednesday nights spent with song and guitar and convivial memories." Since I never saw or heard Latendorf strum a guitar, I shall assume that the musical evenings were reserved for the ladies.

Latendorf's pre-occupation with illustration probably dated from the time he acquired Harper's holdings of drawings the magazine publisher had commissioned of artists from its beginnings some eighty years before. The sale must have occurred in the early 1930s when another dealer, Harry Stone, also purchased the stock of the publishers of *Puck* and *Century Magazine*, which he afterward disposed of in large lots. With no public collecting agencies displaying interest in conserving the archives intact, Latendorf was one of the very few to realize their importance and try to interest private collectors and small museums. Since the Harper collection was particularly strong in Frederic Remington's illustrations, the West in books, painting, sculpture, and illustration became the dominant feature of the business. Teri claimed that Remington was also her first love, and once stated it was her futile search for information about him in the late 1930s that persuaded her to form pictorial reference collections which would demonstrate illustrators' life work year by year. The Remington collection was naturally the first. It comprised nearly three thousand pictures, all assembled from the wood engraved and halftone reproductions extracted from the magazines in which they appeared. The later collections included, among others, the works of Howard Pyle, William T. Smedley, and Peter Newell. About that time she also began to build her private collection of original illustrations. Although she scoured shops for individual drawings, she acquired some material in bulk from the publishers of *Collier's*, the old *Cosmopolitan*, and *Success*, but evidently did not have the means or ready access to major remaining archives. When Teri learned that Scribner still retained a good collection of illustrations it preferred not to sell, she encouraged me to persuade the publisher to present it to the museum at which I curated at the time. That collection is now housed in

"All hands to rescue a derailed electric car ..."
Jay Hambidge • Cat. no. 74

the Cooper-Hewitt Museum (Smithsonian) in New York.

The collection of nearly five thousand drawings for illustrations and cartoons Teri Card accumulated over the years, includes particularly large holdings of individual artists once popular, such as: Palmer Cox (the "Brownie" books), Will Denslow (of "Oz" fame), Charles Jay Taylor, Henry W. McVickar, William L. Jacobs, and Wallace Morgan. Provenance is not always easy to trace, but I know that most of Walter King Stone's drawings came from the estate of the writer, Walter Pritchard Easton, whose works he illustrated almost exclusively. At another time she acquired a significant collection of Arthur Burdett Frost's illustrations from his family. A considerable amount of the material at the Glenbow Museum must also include the collection Teri came into

possession of after Walter Latendorf's death in 1957. At that time she inherited one-third of his estate and ultimately the bookshop and its contents. She operated the shop with her sister ("The Princess") for several years under the name The Latendorf Bookshop. His holdings were also strong in Stone, as well as Lester Hornby, Charles Livingston Bull, Bruce Horsfall, Frank Schoonover, Jay Hambidge, and Howard Pyle.

In the years following 1957, Teri continued Latendorf's practice of issuing periodic sales catalogues, but her publications, which she called "Latendorfers," were actually more scholarly projects. The 176-page Howard Pyle catalogue, which she dedicated "To the True American Spirit," contained an important bibliographical checklist, as well as the usual price list of books, drawings, paintings, and posters. It represented not only the large collection Latendorf had formed from the time he acquired the Harper stock, with eventual publication of this kind in mind, but also the important Pyle originals Teri had carefully gathered herself. That catalogue, and the successful sale that resulted from it, accounts for the lack of original drawings by Pyle in the Glenbow collection.

A native of New England, Teri followed Maxfield Parrish's example when she acquired some two hundred acres of farm land and a cottage in Springfield, Vermont, actually not very far from Parrish's home at Windsor. She apparently thought of it as a future permanent home, a refuge from the crowded city and an ideal place in which to recover her health, much as Parrish had done earlier. To make a necessary modernization of the cottage, which she promptly named

Illustration House, Teri continued to produce on order the pictorial reference collections, as well as now taking on an increased variety of other research and cataloguing projects, all related to illustration. One unique enterprise she devised consisted of persuading large commercial firms like White Rock, the sparkling water people, to commission her to research and document its advertising history. In this instance, I remember her delight when I presented her with John Henry Moser's original design for one of the scantily-clad White Rock girls.

Teri firmly believed that her reference collections would also go a long way toward rescuing some of the illustrators from obscurity. She quickly discovered, during the course of her investigation, how few professional illustrators earned lasting fame and fortune in their lifetimes, that most often enjoyed only a very brief

"The Tournament at Pentecost was at its height."
Clara Elsene Williams Peck • Cat. no. 107

moment in the limelight, usually ending their lives in poverty. How deeply the recurrence of such cases affected her is shown in the following excerpt from a letter written in 1954:

> I found out who I.W. Taber [Isaac Walton Taber] was. He is a puzzle to me, he never would register his name or anything. I wonder if he were an unwanted child... In his old age his eyesight failed him and [he] couldn't work any more; he lived in New York and then broke his leg, and there's no record of his death that I've found, that was around 1930. It does wound pathetic, for the end of a very popular illustrator, doesn't it? Like John Alonzo Williams who died in a charity bed on Welfare Island, and other cases I could mention, like Reginald Birch.

When she discovered Clara Elsene Peck living in near poverty, she befriended her and tried to restore her confidence and pride by offering to purchase her remaining collection of drawings. The more than one hundred drawings, representing a rich archive of Peck's work, is now in the Glenbow Museum collection.

Teri's taste in illustration inclined strongly toward subjects representing fashionable society at ease, romantic fiction, and wholesome good humour, characteristics that echo her own personality. She disliked anything relating to the seamy side of human life and activity, in particular subjects depicting social unrest and the horrors of war. Like Latendorf, she never fully realized how effective illustration could be as a means of communicating vital social and political issues, as indeed it did before and during World War One. They could not understand why I regarded illustrators among the Eight — Luks, Sloan, Glackens, and Shinn — and those like David and Robinson, who contributed to the radical socialist paper *The Masses*, so important. Here is what Teri had to say about Boardman Robinson on one occasion:

> I am sorry to say, I never liked Boardman Robinson's work, I have a couple around here somewhere, and shall be glad to make a present of them to you if I can find them. They are well drawn but always seem to me so macabre and sinister, or pre-occupied with the horrors of war, that I always put them back on the shelf face down. You know me, I like Queen Anne's lace and weathered shingles.

I was making some discoveries of my own those days, and swapping stories with Teri. The following is a rather typical anecdote she related about an original illustration by Edward W. Kemble she had acquired:

> I'm glad you like the Handkerchief Pedlar — I was sure excited when I found it, in an antique shop in Newport, in a dirty old frame and all that. Shop-people are funny, it was an Armenian girl who was very suspicious and reluctant and asked me if I was an antique dealer, and put very high prices on anything I admired; and then when I turned up my nose at this dirty old drawing (to her) gave it to me, for, I think, seven dollars. Such is a traders' lot.

I am particularly nostalgic about the weekend I spent with Teri Card and Walter Latendorf at Illustration House in the summer of 1956, a few weeks before I was scheduled to leave for California to assume a teaching post at UCLA. I did not realize then that it would be the last time the three of us would ever spend together. I still recall Teri as she greeted us on our arrival from the open porch of her immaculate white frame house with its distinctive attic gable. We visited several fascinating places by day, the most memorable for me being a stop at Maxfield Parrish's studio home. Evenings were spent at the house, generally in the open where Walter, playing host, prepared food over a campfire, western-style, and afterward entertained us with song and tall stories.

Teri always gave me free access to the collections exhibited in the house and stored in the barn. Only a relatively small selection could be seen in the house at any one time, usually favourites like Smedley, Parrish, and Frost. I remember seeing an impressive painting by Norman Rockwell for a *Saturday Evening Post* Christmas cover Teri told me came from a trade-off with Rockwell for some of his early drawings in her collection. A splended, large watercolour by Arthur Burdett Frost, featuring a crowing rooster, dominated the breakfast-room and one of the guest-rooms, in this case Walter's, was appropriately decorated with western artifacts and illustrations. To commemorate this visit, he brought a Russell bronze as a house gift. Having good reason to remind herself of my personal interest in Mary Hallock Foote, the first woman illustrator of the West, Teri positioned her only drawing by Foote strategically in my room on a small easel. The major part of the collection was housed in the barn, crammed into cabinet drawers and classified in a system known only to Teri, who acted as curator and conservator.

Although almost thirty years have gone by, I can still conjure up a vivid picture of Teri calling the chipmunks in early morning to feed from her hand, and I can still hear the sound of hearty laughter of my special friends. An intuitive Teri was to write shortly after that last visit — "Come back some day. You can see life isn't going to be long enough."

Maurice Bloch

[Surprised man]
Ernest George Fosbery • Cat. no. 58

INTRODUCTION

nclude at least one romance story, an adventure yarn, and a murder mystery; mix into that format provocative personality profiles, exotic travelogues, humorous farces, useful "how-to" articles, and noteworthy news stories. Such was the formula for the popular and profitable periodical at the turn of the century. The whole issue was then richly illustrated by artists with fresh, innovative styles. Between the years 1890 and 1925 the North American public was eager for this kind of entertaining, informative reading material, and hundreds of publishers were equally enthusiastic to meet that demand.

Several conditions led to the success and popularity of illustrated periodicals and books. First, there was a general economic stability and prosperity in America that resulted in a new, affluent middle class. Secondly, literacy was nearly universal in middle-income families. Also, more leisure was available because of shorter working hours and new labour-saving inventions in the home and work place. Finally, the improvements in printing technology made it possible for publishers to print quality books and periodicals for wide distribution.

[Older and younger women meeting in kitchen]
Frank Bird Masters • Cat. no. 96

Harper's Monthly was an illustrated periodical first published in the 1850s, and its success led *Scribner's* and *Century* to establish similar serials in the 1870s and 1880s. All three became magazines of distinction and elegance. Their publishers employed imaginative illustrators and the best engravers and printers working in America. By the 1880s there were hundreds of periodical titles available, but these three led the way in taste and style.

Harper's, Scribner's, and *Century*, however, cost twenty-five to thirty-five cents per issue, which made them moderately expensive. This led other publishers like Cyrus Curtis, John Brisben Walker, and Robert Collier to cultivate a new body of readers in search of less expensive magazines. If periodicals could be sold for fifteen cents or a dime, these publishers reasoned that middle-class Americans would buy not just one magazine, but several. After all, in the 1890s Americans had entered an era of prosperity and optimism. Salaries were higher than ever, and the cost of living was relatively inexpensive. Education was available for all classes of Americans, resulting in a knowledgeable, informed reading audience. This new audience avidly spent their time and money on inexpensive but entertaining books and magazines.

The popularity of the short story and the novella in America developed because of periodicals. Both literary forms could be read in a sitting. Serialized novels also appeared. Like short stories, they gave the reader just enough to read in one issue, but with an added incentive to purchase future issues of the magazine to finish reading the story. Although some first-rate fiction was published in periodicals, the majority of stories in these early magazines were lighthearted and trivial. Such stories lent themselves nicely to illustration. The pictures added a decorative quality to the magazines, increasing their saleability.

Because periodicals used illustrations so extensively, readers expected illustrations in their books as well. From 1890 to 1920 illustrated fiction had become a fad in America. A few of the bestselling books even reached sales of one million copies — a number staggering to publishers who had never dreamed sales could achieve such heights. In fact, the demand for books was so great, publishers had difficulties keeping bestsellers in print and publishing enough new books to keep their readers satisfied.

Illustrators were in high demand at the beginning of the 1890s. The older periodicals had a staff of artists to do the illustrating; but suddenly there was a demand for so many pictures that art editors spent a good deal of their time reviewing portfolios of eager, young artists just out of art school. It was difficult to break into the top periodicals, but once an illustrator had established his name, he was rarely out of work. And the demand for good pictures meant the pay was high. The average illustrator earned four thousand dollars a year, enough to afford a moderately nice house and a servant. Popular illustrators earned ten thousand to seventy-five thousand dollars making them wealthy by the standards of the day.

The rapid industrialization following the U.S. Civil War produced many new American products. By the turn of the century America was well on its way toward rampant consumerism. The periodical was the perfect place for advertising these goods. Revenue from the advertisers made the production of the dime and fifteen-cent magazine possible. Advertisers also found themselves in a position to influence the format of the magazine. When better paper was available for printing illustrations, for example, advertisers pressured some publishers to pay the extra expense to print their advertisements on the better quality paper. The larger format adopted by *Collier's* and *Ladies' Home Journal* was a direct result of advertisers wanting to run bigger ads.

The technology used in printing illustrations was also a factor in their increased popularity. Halftones would reproduce any medium. This gave the artist variety from the tedium of line cuts. Improvements in colour printing added an enormous boost to the appeal of illustrations as well. The use of rotary presses meant that illustrations could be printed in a fraction of the time older presses had taken. More illustrations could be used because of the speed and cheapness of printing halftones on cylindrical plates. With this new technology, the quality of illustrations improved, demonstrating visually richer texture and a greater variety in style and medium.

In order to understand the status of reproductive printing processes in 1890, however, it is helpful to look briefly at techniques used in the eighteenth and early nineteenth centuries. The very earliest books and periodicals in America employed one of three techniques for reproductive illustrations — woodcuts, wood engravings or copper plate engravings. Woodcuts were more commonly used because they were less expensive to produce and to print. A woodcut is a relief printing process which means it is compatible with type. For example, a page could be set with type and illustrations, and then both could be printed off the same press.

Wood engravings gained in popularity after 1830. They were similar to woodcuts but were executed on harder wood, using fine tools, similar to those of the copper plate engraver. The hardness of the wood allowed the engraver to make more detailed, finer lines. Boxwood

"You derned fool! If you do me out of the sale of land..."
Otto Lang • Cat. no. 91

"A Cheerful Loser"
Rose Cecil O'Neill • Cat. no. 105

was frequently used for the block, but the limited dimensions of the box-tree meant that the "embellishments," as wood engravings were often called, were limited to small designs.

Publishers kept a supply of woodcuts and wood engravings in stock to use when a text needed an illustration. Needless to say, the cuts did not always match the story, but publishers found that illustrations sold books, so the practice continued. This was especially true of juveniles' books which required many illustrations to hold children's attention.

In this early period, copperplate engravings were primarily used for illustrations in elegant, expensive books or in scientific books where detailed drawings required the fine-line accuracy of a copperplate print. Engraving and etching on copper demanded a trained craftsman, but the American colonies and early Republic had very few artisans with such refined skills. Also, printing from copperplates required a special copperplate printing press. The plate, inked by hand, gave only one impression after each inking. The process were therefore slow and expensive.

Materials may have been difficult to come by and the training for illustrators limited, but the most troublesome task before 1830, was finding original artwork to copy. The editor of the *New York Magazine* announced that he would gladly publish engravings of American landscapes if artisans would supply him with suitable designs. Until American art developed, the publishers were forced to copy the engravings in British and continental books.

Lithography had been introduced in America in the second decade of the nineteenth century, and was used briefly for book illustrations. But, there was a prevalent attitude that lithography was a "cheap" reproductive method, and the public preferred copperplates or wood engravings. Because copperplate engraving was prohibitively expensive, wood engravings remained the popular medium. Technological developments improved the quality of the wood-engraved illustrations. By the 1860s, double-page wood-engraved illustrations were common in magazines. The boxwood squares were linked together with wooden dowels to increase the size of the engraving. This practice continued through the 1880s.

Photography revolutionized the business of illustration in America. Prior to photography, artist-illustrators had carried on a long "feud" with wood engravers over misrepresentations of drawings and styles. Illustrators usually turned over a drawing to an engraver who then translated it into a wood engraving. Unfortunately, the artists often did not recognize the finished reproductions as being from their drawings, and blamed the engraver. A few artists, like Winslow Homer, drew directly on the block in an attempt to force the engraver to cut his precise drawings. Still, engravers like illustrators, varied in talent and in style, and the conflicts between the two groups persisted. However, by the 1880s drawings were photographed and the negative image transferred directly onto the block. Photography also ended the restrictions on the size of a drawing because photographs of drawings could be enlarged or reduced to fit the block.

Technological advancements made it possible for photographs to be transferred to metal plates and etched directly. In the beginning however, photographically engraved plates were restricted to line drawings. If an artist wished to create tones, his technique was restricted to finely cross-hatched lines. Halftone reproduction however, solved this problem. Halftones allow the illustrator to use the full range of tones between black and white. The halftone works through the use of a screen placed directly in front of the camera lens. The optical glass screen is ruled with a grid pattern as coarse as thirty grids per square inch and up to a fine ruling of one hundred and seventy-five grids per square inch. The screen breaks up a tonal picture into a series of very fine dots. These dots are then etched into a copper or zinc plate for printing. The development of the halftone revolutionized the illustrating business. Artists were free of the pen and ink medium. Illustrators could now take advantage of wash drawings, watercolours, pastels, gouache and even oil paints.

Colour was also a possibility. The halftone screens were used to shoot separate images for yellow, red, blue and black key plates. New techniques for perfect registration of the four plates facilitated the printing of the image. Colour was obviously an expensive undertaking, but as techniques improved, the costs went down. More and more colour appeared in magazines and books.

The public responded enthusiastically to the new, more lavishly illustrated books and magazines. However, publishing a magazine was a financially precarious undertaking. As one author put it: "Probably there are few business enterprises of more hazardous nature than the establishment of an illustrated magazine."[1] Presuming a publisher had a clever idea for a magazine that would potentially attract an audience, he still faced high production costs. These usually outweighed what the publisher was actually able to charge the public. There were fixed costs like fees to the authors, illustrators, editors, engravers and printers. These were the same whether he issued one hundred or one hundred thousand copies. Then there were the actual expenses for paper, presswork and mailing. The larger the subscription, the larger this expense. *Cosmopolitan Magazine* in 1893, for example, estimated that the actual cost per magazine was eighteen cents — more than it sold for on newsstands.

How then was a magazine to stay in business and make a profit? The difference between the publishing costs and an actual profit was supplied by the advertisers. In 1868, *Peterson's Magazine* used twenty-five pages of advertisements in its Christmas issue. The public complained that all the advertisements took away from the space for literary work. To appease the public, the magazine added eight pages of text, keeping the same number of advertisements. From that issue on, advertisers and magazine publishers benefited mutually. In this early period, advertisements were grouped together in either the front or back of the issue, but it was evident that subscribers were reading the ads.

Companies with aggressive ad campaigns saw the benefits of continuous magazine advertising. Most advertisers agreed that the dollars which went into magazine ads paid the highest dividends, thus advertisers competed for the best artists to promote their products. At first, companies handled their own advertising campaigns, but as the business became more complex, agencies were established to negotiate the ads. Illustrators benefited from this trend, because advertisers generally paid higher prices than publishers. Some of these images became classics. Leyendecker created the sophisticated American man for Arrow Shirts; Jessie Willcox Smith drew the tender mother and child at bathtime for Ivory Soap; and Rose O'Neill originated the chubby-cheeked children eating JELL-O brand gelatin.

Advertisers dreamed up many gimmicks to lure potential customers. Armour Beef Extract, for example, offered calendars each year featuring the "pretty girl" faces by some of America's top illustrators. Box tops, soap wrappers, and extract labels could be redeemed for reproductions of illustrator art. Even magazines offered their own premiums for artwork in exchange for new subscriptions.

"A Dutch Kitchen"
George Wharton Edwards • Cat. no. 51

The popular illustrators of this era reaped the benefits of all this exposure. *Life* and *McClure's* included short biographies and pictures of their top illustrators. *Collier's* promoted coming issues with promises of cover art or inside illustrations of favourite illustrators who now had the status of celebrities. The publisher was the primary patron for the arts in America. Thus, this era was deservedly called "the golden age of American illustration."

In the 1880s, the art departments at the large publishing houses were made up of an art director and a small, but select coterie of illustrators. At Harper and Brothers there were Charles Parsons, art editor, and his "discoveries," such as Frederic Remington, Howard Pyle, Edwin Austin Abbey, Arthur Burdett Frost, and William T. Smedley. These artists worked at desks spread out in the same room. Close friendships developed between the men as they helped and criticized each other's work. They did not work from models, but from their imaginations and from extensive clipping files that they shared.

The illustrator George Wharton Edwards recounted an anecdote that helped change this system. In American art schools the standard academic training of an artist required tedious hours of drawing from plaster casts to learn the proportions and anatomy of the human body before advancing to life classes. European schools, on the other hand, taught life drawing through using live models from the beginning of a student's training. American artists of the nineteenth century ventured to the art academies of Paris, Munich, Antwerp, and London, and returned to America accustomed to drawing from live models. One such young illustrator approached the art editor of a major publication house and requested a model for an illustration assignment he had received. The surprised editor, knowing models were expensive to hire, told him that illustrators were expected to work from their visual memories, not to rely on models. But the artist persisted and only a few weeks later he was drawing from a live model in a studio away from the publication house. Soon other assignments were given on a freelance basis, and the art department with its stable of illustrators was broken up. One advantage for the publisher issuing work on a freelance basis was that he was neither responsible for the costs of hiring models nor for keeping clipping files. This now became the illustrator's responsibility. The demand for artwork was so great that publication houses could not afford to keep enough artists on staff. By hiring freelance, houses could also change illustrators frequently, thereby introducing new styles as well as patronizing well established ones. Illustrators benefited in turn by being able to accept assignments from different publishers. For female artists it was especially beneficial because they could then pursue illustration careers and stay home with their families.

Although individual publishers might vary slightly in their methods, the procedure of producing an illustrated magazine was basically the same from house to house. The art editor received a schedule of stories from the editor about three to four months in advance of publication. (With the weeklies, the time was shortened considerably.) This schedule outlined the advertisements, reviews, short stories, serials, and articles by numbers of pages of text and illustration. The art editor was responsible for selecting the illustrators he felt suited each item. He also secured photographs and technical diagrams. If the actual manuscripts were available at this date, they too were sent to the art editor. Authors were notorious for not meeting deadlines, so if the manuscript was not available, illustrators were sent an abstract of the story.

After the art editor had read all the stories and articles, he made a list of the illustrators he considered suited to each article. A few illustrators at the very top were busy enough to turn down work or needed more notice than some art editors could give. Art editors worked with very tight deadlines and favoured illustrators who worked quickly and got their pictures in on time. They also preferred illustrators who had built reputations as specialists. Charles Livingston Bull, for example, was known for his animal illustrations; Henry Hutt was a "pretty girl" artist, and Albert Wenzell, a delineator of the "smart set." These specializations were considered by the art editor as he selected artists for various assignments. The art editor was always available for meeting new, aspiring illustrators who came *en masse*, portfolio in hand. Although the percentage of illustrators who made it into the leading magazines was small in comparison to those who tried, almost every illustrator experienced that first "cold call" on an art editor and the thrill of an unexpected sale.

Upon receiving the assignment, the illustrators were free to work in the method best-suited to their work habits. They were given manuscripts and deadline dates. Some art editors designed the page format, but most left these decisions to the illustrators. After 1920, this practice changed, with the art editor taking responsibility for the page design. The illustrator was told how many illustrations were needed, the space allowed for the illustrations in relation to the text, and if colour was to be used. The early generation of illustrators had been told by art editors what scenes to illustrate, but by 1900 this decision was almost always left to the illustrator.

The first illustration for a serial was the most important. It introduced the characters, set the mood of the story, and caught the attention of a potential reader. The second and third illustrations enhanced the text but never revealed the dénouement. The authors' biggest complaint against illustrators was directed towards those who revealed too much of the story. Illustrations, authors said, were intended to interpret the text. Those illustrators who gave away the plot were accused of nothing short of plagiarism by the authors.

Authors also complained that illustrators did not read the text they were illustrating. There was a group of readers — the "mistake finders" — whose greatest pleasure was finding the mistakes illustrators had made. One of the more serious mistakes a reader detected arose when an illustrator, faced with a character whose name could have been either male or female, drew a male. A more careful reading indicated that "he" was clearly a "she." Letters poured into the editor regarding this blunder. On another occasion, an outraged author published a letter he had received from an illustrator. The illustrator wrote: "I have been appointed to make the pictures for your interesting story. I can make the final picture much more effective if you will change the storm with which you close into a peaceful sunset."[2] Needless to say the author kept his ending. Drawing a blonde heroine when she was described as having long brown hair, mounting a horse from the wrong side, and milking a cow in an incorrect way were more typical of the mistakes readers found. Art directors forwarded these letters to the illustrator, who was expected to answer them personally.

Correctness in costume was always important, both in accurate historical costumes and keeping *au courant* with contemporary dress. As a whole, illustrators took great pains to avoid mistakes. Edwin Austin Abbey was an avid costume collector. He often paid half the price he received for a drawing to purchase the costumes he needed. If he could not find the exact costume for a period piece, he paid to have it made based on old prints or paintings. Howard Chandler Christy would occasionally hire a seamstress to work in his studio as he painted, altering the costume to fit his exact wishes and the dictates of fashion. An illustrator, faced with drawing a female character who carried a "white fascinator" against her light-coloured gown, could not achieve the contrast he needed for a good reproduction. He telegraphed the author, "May Mary carry a dark shawl?" The author humorously admitted that the telegram confused him. He wrote: "[it was] one of the most bewildered moments of my life. Recovering as I slowly identified Mary, I changed the text gladly, and Mary stands, a joy forever, her shawl over her arm."[3] In another example, Frederick Yohn was assigned a story that took place in the backwoods of Kentucky. Not being familiar with the area, he visited the mountain people and lived with them. He wanted to take costumes from the people, but found them quite reluctant to part with any articles of clothing. He even offered to buy them new clothes in exchange for the old, and a few obliged. The clothes were so ragged and filthy that Yohn's wife insisted that they be washed before he could bring them into the house. Washing such "treasures" was out of the question. A compromise was reached in airing them on the clothes line.

Accuracy, however, was not always the aim of the art editor. Often the priority was to provide a glamorous and sophisticated tone through illustrations. In one case, an illustrator was given a story that dealt with the actors of vaudeville. The illustrator moved into a boarding house where a troupe of performers lived, and spent two weeks observing and sketching the entertainers. He then proudly displayed his finished works before the art editor who was less than pleased. The subjects were not attractive models, but realistic people taken from direct observation. The editor accused the illustrator of knowing nothing about vaudeville performers. The deadline in this instance was past, so the illustrations ran, but the illustrator was told that his drawings would be more carefully supervised in the future.

Commercialism was the bane of the illustrators' art. Too often art editors desired "images" rather than a truthful portrayal of a subject. The illustrator was caught between what the public wanted to see and his own artistic endeavours. Artists may have been discontented with art editors, but editors too had their frustrations with certain artists. In one case, Frederico Gruger was asked to draw a bracelet for the story "The Bracelet" by Robert Hichens. He protested that he did not draw bracelets, but would oblige this one time. When he sent the drawing to the art editor, he included a witty letter of things he would not draw:

> Here is a list of things I can't draw and by all that's Holy, I won't even try:
> Policemen, army officers, dogs, automobiles, bracelets, golfsticks, golf players, postmen, messenger boys, smart ladies, smart gentlemen, new furniture (especially white, with Duco finish). There are several others.
> These others I forget at the moment but will recognize on sight. I know their faces but forget their names. [4]

"She sat in silence watching him..."
Lucius Wolcott Hitchcock • Cat. no. 80

Most authors of popular fiction in American periodical literature used the same monotonous story lines over and over. Likewise, illustrators who were given the task of illustrating countless "he and she" pictures, were faced with the temptation to repeat successful compositions and scenery. Sid Hydeman, art editor for *Redbook*, suggested that it was unwise for illustrators to pick the obvious subject of a story to illustrate. If the story was about horseracing, for example, he advised that the illustrator not draw a picture of the actual race, but rather the moments before or after the race. He also protested that it was nearly impossible to draw an imaginative "boy-girl" picture, especially if the author called for the couple to stare dreamily at each other over a restaurant table. Hydeman urged his illustrators to portray other elements of these romantic yarns and to avoid the stale, well-worn images.

Many illustrators, however, were entrapped by formalized devices of drawing and composition. As critic Charles H. Caffin observed: "...what started with being originality has become stereotyped by repetition. The beau becomes more square and rigid, the girl's sweetness drawn out longer and longer until the figure and suggestion of life are buried in an avalanche of frou-frou. Finally, like the Cheshire cat, the original 'girl and beau' have vanished except for the vacuity of their facial expressions."[5]

Max Eastman, editor of *The Masses*, described the following formulas that the unimaginative artists used to evoke certain sentimental emotions:

Wistfulness in a pretty girl — indicated by arching her eyebrows clear up into her hair.
Adventurous altho stylish athletism in a young man — indicated in the jaw and pants.
Romance in the meeting of the two — indicated by his gazing upon the earth, she upon infinity.
Pathos of old age — indicated with bending knees or a market basket.
Sweet and divine innocence of children — usually indicated in the stockings.[6]

Eastman did not place all the blame on the illustrator for the commercialism of illustration. He also pointed out that art editors shared the blame because most were not willing to let illustrators experiment with new styles and subject matters.

The cover design was the most important illustration on both magazine and book covers. As the book trade put it "a novel must wear its heart on its jacket." The older, more established serials like *Scribner's* and *Century* did not use pictorial material on their covers. Each had a decorative border design on a standard colour paper that was used on every issue. Other magazines such as *The Smart Set* used the same pictorial cover for each issue so that the purchaser would have no difficulty recognizing the magazine on the newsstand. *Ladies' Home Journal* was the first major magazine to change the cover for each issue. Other periodicals followed its example and established themes on their covers. *McClure's* and *Cosmopolitan* always ran "pretty girl" pictures. *Good Housekeeping* had an exclusive contract with Jessie Willcox Smith to feature her illustrations of idealized children on each cover. The *Saturday Evening Post, Success,* and *Life*, for example, changed the cover and theme each month. Subjects were often seasonal, such as a Christmas theme for the December issue, and an Easter subject for April. "Story pictures" of human interest were also common. *Ladies' Home Journal* paid the artist John Singer Sargent one thousand dollars to feature his elegant portrait of Ethel Barrymore on one of its covers. It did not sell well. Seemingly, the American reading public was less interested in fine art on covers, than it was in the more popular "smart" pictures.

The art critic, Thomas Craven, commented:
the covers of the popular magazines were be-slobbered with faces of every description — wistful seducers, pouting dimpled rustics, virginal co-eds, metropolitan parasites with a flashing smile and high-light on every tooth — all of them stupidly drawn and offensive to readers of any taste.[7]

He was not alone in his opinion. Another author wrote:
'The Gibson Girl,' 'The Christy Girl,' 'The Stanslaws Girl,' 'The Harrison Fisher Girl' — these are features to be advertised on the front cover. And yet, what is the advertisement, but an obituary notice of these men as artists? It certifies that they have given up their profession of realizing in line the varieties of life's experiences, and gone into the manufacturing business. They are now turning out an article that will sell widely in competition, because it is modeled strictly on the lines here indicated; and while they may find it profitable to vary the model a little from year to year, as progressive manufacturers do, the main lines were laid down in the first big sale and no risks will be taken.[8]

The realist illustrator Morgan Wallace offered the same protest from the illustrator's viewpoint when he wrote:
...the pretty girl... is one of the curses of the modern age. She started out as a mushy magazine cover, and spread out through the whole

28

world of American illustration, so that no one now can draw a really beautiful woman or a woman of character or any humor.[9]

Magazine publishers spent both time and money on full-colour reproductions for covers. When colour printing became popular, there was a tendency among publishers to use a lot of colour rather than a little because the cost was virtually the same. In time, art editors abandoned the gaudy, ornate covers using colour in moderation and good taste instead. A few magazines used a somewhat tedious repetition of subject matter. But others such as the *Saturday Evening Post* and *Life* featured a great variety of subjects and styles, and created memorable images of American life at the turn of the century.

If a book cover was to have an illustration, publishers often used a four-colour reproduction glued to a full cloth binding. It was common to have the picture framed with a gold-embossed design in an Art Nouveau or Arts and Crafts style. End papers were also specially designed for the paste-down and the flyleaves. The decorative theme was sometimes carried throughout the book in chapter headings and page borders. Illustrators occasionally designed the bindings and decorations, but usually the decorations were assigned to artists who specialized in that area. Book decorations were so popular from 1890 to 1920, that both the illustrator and decorator were often given credit on the title page. However, after World War One, illustrated book jackets replaced decorative book bindings.

When the art editor received the finished illustrations for a story and had given them his approval, they were photostated or blueprinted. They were then reduced or enlarged to the size they would appear in the publication. The art editor then made a dummy page, pasted in the prints, and examined the layout. The most common page design had either a square or a vignette picture that bled into the text so that the margins of text framed the picture. A square-up or split centre meant the picture was divided in half. An artist based his composition on that fact, allowing one-quarter inch margins to form the gutter of the book or magazine. Experienced illustrators kept the page design in mind. If a picture was to appear in the upper right-hand corner of the page, the action of the picture had to face left and down so that the picture would not seem to be heading off the page. May Wilson Preston, one of the leading illustrators at the turn of the century, took an old magazine and found a page with similar layout to the one with which she was working. She cut out the illustration and carefully pasted one of her rough sketches into the void to test her composition in relation to the page design.

When she had selected the most suitable composition, she finished the work.

After 1920, the style of layout design changed in most magazines. Art editors took control of designing the page before the illustrations were assigned to illustrators. Prior to this, illustrators had control over page design. As Wallace Morgan saw it:

[this change] made it necessary for men to force their compositions into all sorts of strange shapes and sizes, and thereby hampered the full expression of ideas, and made it almost impossible to fill some of these spaces with a picture that was really an illustration. So the emphasis came to be more on the decorative quality than on the illustrative quality... The result was that the part of the story that was to be illustrated was given to you, and the shape it was to appear in was given to you, and the medium it was to appear in was given to you, and everybody began to work for the business office, and the editorial office, instead of expressing themselves.[10]

After the blueprint dummy was arranged, the works were sent to photographers. They were either photographed through screens for a halftone or photographed for a zinc plate if the work was a line drawing. The halftone reduced the clarity of the original by about twenty per cent. This meant that illustrators needed to include sharp contrasts and strong outlines in the original. The original drawing was only valuable insofar as a good photograph could be taken from it; therefore, artists were free to change the composition by whiting out areas and re-drawing them. Smaller errors were corrected with erasures or scraping out a line with a blade. Major changes often involved pasting a clean white scrap of paper over an area to re-work a character or scene. Although these corrections may have looked messy to the eye, the camera lens would not have detected them.

Illustrators were aware that most of their works would survive only as reproductions; therefore, their reputations were made by the reproduction, not by the original. A photograph was mechanically transferred to a metal plate, but an engraver still needed to sharpen lines and accent highlights. The same old arguments among artist, engraver and printer existed then. Although the reproductions were certainly closer to the originals than they had been twenty-five years earlier, artists continued to blame the engraver or the printer if their work came out muddy or blotchy. Engravers and printers, on the other hand, were trained craftsmen and could turn a mediocre drawing into a decent reproduction. They

"It is a pity you cannot smoke, Michael."
Elizabeth Shippen Green • Cat. no. 69

argued that if illustrators were more knowledgeable about the potential of modern printing processes, their drawings would greatly benefit in reproduction.

When illustrators sold drawings to publishers before 1900, they sold the reproduction rights and the drawings. After the originals had been photographed, they had little or no value to either the illustrators or publishers. The drawings were sometimes filed away for future use in advertising or used as part of a clipping file for reference. Publishers periodically destroyed the filed originals to make room to store others. It was that practice that makes original drawings for book and periodical illustration before 1900 so scarce today.

The illustrators, however, were gaining in status and recognition. Illustrators in the 1890s were beginning to receive fan mail from readers requesting the purchase of the drawing for a specific illustration. Illustrators were obliged to turn over the requests to the publishers, who were usually glad to sell to the public. *Puck Magazine* ran an ad in 1900 offering to sell any drawing in the magazine if the reader would send the issue and page number. Prices were quoted to the inquirer by mail and the sale made. It was obviously successful because shortly after this offer, they advertised a gallery in the *Puck* building where the public could view and purchase originals. Although there are no records of *Puck's* sales, based on the policies of other publishers at this time, it is unlikely that the artists received any royalties.

In 1900, a group of illustrators met to discuss these practices and other complaints they had with publishers. In 1901, they formed the Society of Illustrators. William T. Smedley was its first president, and a few of the original members were N.C. Wyeth, Charles Dana Gibson, William Glackens, and Everett Shinn. The organization was informal at first, but became incorporated in 1921. Women were admitted as associate members in 1905 and full members after 1921. The members met as friends and colleagues to share experiences regarding the making and selling of their works.

Prices paid to illustrators varied, depending on the illustrator's reputation and the art work.[11] Robert Blum was paid one hundred and fifteen dollars for each drawing in the well-known series "Japonica," which appeared in *Scribner's* in 1891. Scribner's also paid for Blum's trip to Japan with author Edwin Arnold. "Japonica" was issued as a book as well, but there is no record that Blum was paid for book reproductions. Also, some of the drawings for "Japonica" were sold. Frederick Yohn and Arthur Burdett Frost, both fellow illustrators, purchased the drawings from Scribner's, but there was no indication in the Scribner's files that Blum received any com-

mission from that sale. After about 1903, contracts with artists usually stated whether or not they would receive "portfolio rights," entitling them to additional money if the works were published in a promotional publication.

Illustrators established their own individual contracts with publishers. In 1913, Paul Bransom did thirteen drawings for the book *Wind in the Willows* and was paid eight hundred dollars. In 1914, William J. Aylward did a series of yachting pictures in *Scribner's* and was paid two hundred dollars for each. Scribner's kept the originals. In 1920, Arthur Burdett Frost did four drawings for *The Trials of Jonathan Goode* (cat. no. 60) and was paid two hundred dollars for the four.

Walter Appleton Clark agreed that all drawings he had done for *Scribner's* before 1900 could be sold if half the proceeds came to him. All of Clark's drawings after 1901 were to be returned to the artist. George Wharton Edwards received a twenty-five per cent commission on all drawings sold by Scribner's. Harrison Fisher did a calendar of "pretty girls" for the publisher in 1905 and was paid one hundred dollars for each watercolour. The drawings remained with Scribner's for one year. Half the sale price from those sold went to Fisher. In 1903, the agreement with Frank Vincent Dumond states that the artist "is to have the privilege of buying back any of his drawings made for us at twenty-five dollars each. We shall consult him before selling any of his work." Jessie Willcox Smith agreed with Scribner's to illustrate a Kipling book for two hundred dollars per drawing. Her agreement was that "ownership [was] to be decided later and to cost an additional sum, 'probably considerable.' " She was correct; the drawings were sold for three hundred dollars each after their publication. N.C. Wyeth illustrated *Westward Ho!* for thirty-five hundred dollars and the paintings sold for two hundred to four hundred dollars each. Stanley Arthurs' contract included "portfolio rights." He was paid a ten per cent royalty if the drawings were used again. If no portfolio was published, Arthurs was free to publish the drawings elsewhere.

Other artists did not negotiate such good deals. E.M. Ashe sold a drawing to Scribner's for thirty-nine dollars, and five months later Scribner's sold it for twenty-five dollars. No royalties went to the artist.

The more status an illustrator had, the easier it was for him to negotiate a good agreement. Gibson, for example, was in such great demand that *Collier's* lured him away from *Life* with a one hundred thousand dollar contract to do one hundred drawings over a four-year period. At the height of his popularity, Harrison Fisher was paid three thousand dollars per magazine cover illustration. Illustrators were encouraged to take exclusive contracts with top magazines for the security of

"One method"
Rose Cecil O'Neill • Cat. no. 106

steady work. Elizabeth Shippen Green, for example, had an exclusive contract with Harper's from 1902 to 1911.

Illustrators also supplemented their incomes with other kinds of work. Oberhardt did portrait paintings of famous Americans. Robert Blum, Albert Wenzell, Will Hicok Low, and Walter Shirlaw were muralists. Many illustrators taught at art schools and academies.

There were only a few good art schools in the United States, and students from all over the country went to them. In New York there were: the Art Students' League, the National Academy of Design, The Cooper Union Art School, the New York School of Art, and the

Metropolitan Museum School. William Merritt Chase had an experimental summer school on Long Island. Students lived at his home in Shinnecock Hills and studied and drew outdoors. In Philadelphia there were: the Pennsylvania Academy of the Fine Arts, the Spring Garden Institute, Drexel Institute, and the Philadelphia School of Design for Women. Howard Pyle had his famous "school" of individually selected students at Chadds Ford, Pennsylvania. In Washington, D.C. there was the Corcoran School. In Boston there were the Museum of Fine Arts School, the Cowles Art School and artist Eric Pape took private students. In the Midwest there were: the John Herron Art Institute in Indianapolis, the Art Institute of Chicago, the McMicken School of Design in Cincinnati, and the St. Louis School of Fine Arts. The Mark Hopkins Institute of Art was in San Francisco. After studying in the United States, many illustrators went to Europe to finish their education. Independent schools such as Colarossi and Julian's in Paris were popular as were art academies in Antwerp, London and Munich.

Most students in art schools did not train to be illustrators — they were simply studying art. After graduating they found that illustrating for major periodicals was a good way to earn some money while pursuing the "fine arts" of painting or printmaking. However, as illustrators earned more and more money, many students decided to train specifically as illustrators. Art schools began to include courses on illustration as part of their curriculum. N.C. Wyeth commented on this trend in an article on the state of illustration in America. He held that one cannot "learn" illustration. Instead, one must study art and find that "art and life are incorporate." If one is a good artist, Wyeth felt, it follows that one will be a good illustrator. He detested the gimmicks that many young illustrators used to sell a drawing to a publisher. As Wyeth put it:

> The fact is the student is inclined and encouraged to look upon the phenomena of life as merely fit or unfit material with which to construct clever pictures. The result: they never reach the point where the creation of a picture becomes a constitutional necessity, but rather amounts to a mere intellectual attainment — the one vital, the other ephemeral. To unfold to the young mind the glory of all facts of existence should be the fundamental function of the art school, but in just this they are utterly deficient.[12]

Many friendships were established between illustrators during their school days. Illustrators shared studio space, helped each other secure assignments, and encouraged each others' artistic talents. When the Society of Illustrators was established, it was intended as an organization in which illustrators discussed the business aspects of their careers, but it also provided a social atmosphere for illustrators and encouraged good friendships between artists. The society had meetings, parties, and an annual costume ball that functioned also as a fund-raiser. Author Julian Street described these galas as great fun. He wrote: "The shows and parties given by the authors are uniformly awful, but the shows and parties of the illustrators are so good that even the attendance of authors in large numbers cannot spoil them."[13] The society also helped illustrators organize their war efforts in 1917.

Other organizations drew illustrators together as well. The Franklin Inn Club was established in Philadelphia in 1902 to bring together authors, illustrators, editors, and publishers. Although authors and publishers far outnumbered the illustrators, it encouraged awareness of issues and concerns between publishing professionals. Illustrators Howard Pyle, Thornton Oakley, George Harding, and George Gibbs were a few of the members.

In New York there were many clubs, societies, and meeting places for the artistic community. There was the Salamungdi Club, the Lamb's Club, the Watercolour Society, the Tile Club, and the Dutch Treat Club. In the second decade of the twentieth century the Café François was a popular restaurant where illustrators met. Many lived in the suburbs of New York City. Edmund Ashe, George Wright, Henry Patrick Raleigh, Arthur Dove, John Held, Rose O'Neill, and Ernest Fuhr were all neighbours and friends in Westport, Connecticut. Edmund Ashe was instrumental in establishing the Knocker's Club where artists, playwrights, authors, actors, and actresses met to "knock" each others' works with constructive criticism. The club was also the basis of the Silvermine Artists' Guild, an art school and colony which still exists today in Norwalk, Connecticut.

Female illustrators were often restricted from membership in these clubs. There were, however, many close friendships between the women. Charlotte Harding and Alice Barber Stephens for example, shared a studio. Violet Oakley, Jessie Willcox Smith, and Elizabeth Shippen Green rented co-operatively an estate they called Cogslea outside Philadelphia. Green's marriage broke up that trio, but Smith and Oakley spent their entire lives together. The female artists in Philadelphia established their own club — the Plastic Club. Jessie Willcox Smith, Elizabeth Shippen Green, Florence S. Stilwell, May Wilson Preston, Gertrude Kay, and Blanche Fisher Greer were a few of the female

"Now I guess we understand each other..."
Ernest Fuhr • Cat. no. 63

illustrators who belonged to the club. The Plastic Club held an annual exhibition devoted exclusively to the work of female illustrators. It also arranged lectures by such noted authorities as William Merritt Chase and Alfonz Mucha.

The exhibitions of American illustrations organized by clubs and societies generated an interest in the original drawings of illustrator art. Edward Bok, editor of the *Ladies' Home Journal*, sponsored an exhibition in 1895 of two hundred and fifty original illustrations that had appeared in the magazine. The public was invited to choose its ten favorite works, and the winners were published in a portfolio on good quality paper, suitable for framing. The *Journal* sold two hundred thousand copies of the portfolio. Not only were illustrations a part of America's visual imagery in books and periodicals, but they were also what Americans chose to hang on the walls of their homes. Other exhibitions included: *Collier's*

Collection of Original Drawings and Paintings by Distinguished American Painters and Illustrators (1902); the *Exhibition of Drawings for Newspaper and Book Illustration by Well Known Artists* (1911), sponsored by Jordon Marsh of Boston; and *A Collection of Illustrations by American Artists* (1911), organized by the American Federation of Arts with the help of the Society of Illustrators.

There was an often-quoted statistic in this period that more people saw the works of these illustrator artists than visited the Metropolitan Museum of Art in one year. If a subscription rate of a top periodical was one million with at least two people benefiting from each subscription, plus the number of issues sold on newsstands, each month these artists potentially had a viewing audience of more than two million people. Their objective was to please as many of the viewers as possible without compromising artistic merits.

Illustration was commerical art, done primarily to enhance the sales of a periodical. N.C. Wyeth saw commercialism as a condition of illustration.[14] Even in commercial art, he felt, the artist could paint from a spirit inside himself. Perhaps N.C. Wyeth could. He was successful enough to turn down assignments he did not like or want. When Wyeth read Jules Verne's *20,000 Leagues under the Sea* he wrote to the art editor at *Harper's* that he absolutely had no feeling for the book — worse it disgusted him. He refused to illustrate it.

Other illustrators were not as scrupulous, probably because they were not as popular as Wyeth and were in no position to turn away work. As Will Bradley saw it: "there are still honest and workmanlike men in the field, [however] they are nearly swamped by the hordes of the half-trained, and worse still, unscrupulous illustrators whose sole ambition is to make money easily, spend it freely, and ride about in big motor cars."[15] Harrison Fisher, for example, was not embarrassed in the least by his huge salary and successful illustration career. From a newspaper article came this revealing interview with Fisher:

> He came out from an inner quarter in his shirt sleeves and cigarette and when directly accused of being commercial, laughingly admitted it. "What would you do?" he exclaimed in mock heroics. "Commerical? Of course. I get the last penny out of a picture! So would you. Who would not? My vogue will not last, and I know I improve each passing hour. The Fisher girl is sought to-day. Will she be tomorrow, or who will stay for how long! Therefore, as beseems a man whose ultimate ambition is to become a genuine colorist in the oils, I seize each opportunity to add to the financial earnings of every drawing, so that when I do begin my more serious work I'll have the home, the motor car, and bank account to forfend possible scarcity of orders."
>
> "But there is surely some idealism in your present occupation?" ventured the writer.
>
> "Of a certain sort, yes," responded the illustrator. "From my earliest beginnings in newspaper illustration in San Francisco, I have been convinced, nay, obsessed, that what the public desired most to look at was a pretty girl — and that same fair maid in rightful coloring and not a dreary black and white. I've clung to the idea and thus far I may say that events have proved the wisdom and correctness of my belief.
>
> "No question but that I've been fortunate, yet I have taken no chances with that frail mistress, but like any careful business man have kept my fences in good repair. In other words, realizing that my water colors had an increasing vogue, I have not been satisfied with one price on a drawing, but have seen to it that it gained me three and sometimes four prices.
>
> "For example," said Mr. Fisher, as he walked to a file of drawings stacked against a mantle-piece, near which there was a full-length drawing of a charming girl in colors which he said had been done in exactly eight hours and worth three hundred dollars as it stood for the first sale:
>
> "Here are a lot of girls' heads and full-length drawings in which the girl is ever paramount, which have already been used for color pages to a magazine. I do not sell them outright, and thus they are returned to me. Since their first use they have already appeared in a gift book and my calendar. Some of these have been used as the queens of card packs, and for postal cards. Three more uses still remain. They will go first into a second edition of the gift book with a few new sketches added. Then copies will be struck from them for poster and decorative designs, and finally the originals themselves are sold.
>
> "I am not working as hard as I did a year ago," he continued, "simply because of this vogue. I charge more and work less, which is an excellent philosophy if it works the right way."[16]

"J. Harvey Smith had gazed upon the group for an instant..."
Arthur Garfield Dove • Cat. no. 50

Fisher's ambition to use his commercial success as a beginning to a career as a fine arts painter was also a hope of many other illustrators. Fisher never gained recognition beyond his illustration career, but others did. Arthur Dove, America's first abstract painter, survived the early years of his career by accepting illustration assignments. Edward Hopper did the same. John Sloan, William Glackens, Everett Shinn, and George Luks all illustrated before they achieved recognition as painters and printmakers. Although they felt that illustration was an inferior vocation to fine art painting, none of these men compromised their artistic standards in their illustrations.

Other illustrators experienced the restrictions of commercialism in illustration and endeavoured to rid themselves of thematic repetition. Maxfield Parrish did so many drawings of girls and boys lying on rocks in cool arcadian settings that he tired of the subject. Parrish said, "I've painted them for thirteen years and I could paint them and sell them for thirteen more. That's the peril of the commercial art game. It tempts a man to repeat himself."[17] Even Howard Pyle, who was considered by many as a mentor and leader in American illustration, was riddled with self-doubts about his own artwork and became bored with the monotony of picture-making. He tried an art editor's position with *McClure's* but was not successful. Pyle then turned to mural painting before he died.

The Golden Age of Illustration peaked in 1917. After the war it struggled for a while and then succumbed to mediocrity. Various critics of the day saw different reasons for its demise. Charles Caffin blamed the publishers for under-estimating public tastes and forcing illustrators to work in rigid, proven modes. Thomas Craven pointed to the greed of illustrators whose only concern was making more money. Stanley Arthurs saw the problem resting with the quick tempo of the twentieth century in which everything moved so quickly one did not have the time to do well thought out work. Tudor Jenks, from an author's point of view, believed that the illustrator had become too self-centred. Illustrators, in his opinion, wanted the glory and honour, and were not satisfied to be interpreters of a text. Art editors argued a similar point. Many believed that the new contracts that gave artists ownership of the original art work resulted in artists becoming more interested in the resale value of their work than in the function of the drawings and paintings to illustrate a text. Weitenkampf held that illustrators were merely making pictures in a facile, carefree way, and not considering the harmony of the illustration to the typeface, layout and design of the whole. N.C. Wyeth saw the problem stemming from art schools which ignored the spiritual aspects of being an artist. Julian Street believed that it was not the illustration that was declining, but the writing. Ultimately, an unidentified author wrote in the *Atlantic*, "Blessed be the magazine which does not illustrate its stories."

All of these issues were factors in the decline of illustrated literature, but there were other reasons as well. First, the vogue for lighthearted, entertaining literature dwindled away and realism took its place. Realistic fiction was not well-suited to illustration. Secondly, the public was turning to the motion picture, which had the added novelty of sound for entertainment. Movies replaced illustrations as the primary visual resource of the American public. Radios in every home became the arbiters of news, fads, and fictional stories. Magazines and books began using photography to illustrate their pages rather than drawn or painted illustrations. The only books consistently using artwork were for children. There were illustrators who produced fine illustrations in the decades that followed, but never again did these artists enjoy the high profile status they had known during the years 1890-1925.

NOTES

1. "Illustrated Magazines a Costly Luxury," *Review of Reviews*, vol. 7 (1893), p. 94.
2. "Our Illustrators," *Atlantic Magazine*, vol. 119 (1917), p. 286.
3. "Our Illustrators," p. 285.
4. Sid Hydeman, *How to Illustrate for Money*, (New York, 1936), p. 58.
5. Charles H. Caffin, "A Note on American Illustration," *Independent*, vol. 63 (1907), pp. 1218-19.
6. "Magazine Art in America as Diagnosed by an Impatient Editor," *Current Opinion*, vol. 58 (1915), p. 117.
7. Thomas Craven, "The Decline of Illustration," *American Mercury*, vol. 12 (Oct., 1927), p. 205.
8. Max Eastman, *Journalism Versus Art*, (New York, n.d.), pp. 41-42.
9. Ernest W. Watson, *Forty Illustrators and Their Work*, (New York, 1946), p. 201.
10. Watson, p. 202.
11. All information on fees to illustrators is taken from the Scribner's files, courtesy of the archives of the Brandywine River Museum, Chadds Ford, Pennsylvania.
12. N.C. Wyeth, "For Better Illustration," *Scribner's*, vol. 66 (1919), p. 642.
13. Julian Street, "In Justice to the Illustrators," *The Bookman*, vol. 58 (1923), p. 2.
14. Wyeth, p. 638.
15. Will Bradley, "The Art of Illustration," *The Nation*, vol. 97, p. 42.
16. "Modern Picture Making and Its Generous Rewards — How a Group of Illustrators Is Reaping Fortunes by Drawing Pictures of the Modern Girl," from unidentified newspaper clipping in the Franklin Inn Papers, courtesy of the Pennsylvania Historical Society. Possibly from the *Public Ledger*, c.1910.
17. Susan Meyer, *America's Great Illustrators*, (New York, 1978), p. 124.

THE PERIODICALS

Periodical literature has been an important literary and educational source since colonial times. Early American publishers started several magazines, but many of them failed within a year or two because of competition from cheaper newspapers. Periodicals tried to distinguish themselves from newspapers by presenting their readership with a more elegant publication and providing illustrations. But illustrations were expensive — even one engraved plate could equal the cost of printing the entire issue. In the years after the American Revolution, publishers struggled to find markets within the American public. In doing so, they provided a cultural link between diverse communities within the United States and spread new ideas about the emerging democracy.

"Lena and Billy swarmed into the room without waiting for permission ..."
Ernest Fuhr • Cat. no. 64

By the 1880s, with increased literacy and more leisure for reading, there was a substantial audience for magazines in general, illustrated magazines in particular. Seeking to take advantage of the potential readership, publishers marketed not only general magazines, but also specialized magazines aimed at groups of readers such as women and children. By 1900, there were fifty-five hundred different periodicals available to the American public.[1] Circulation for popular magazines in the early 1890s were nearing one hundred thousand — a number which seemed phenomonal to the publishers. That number multiplied ten-fold in the first two decades of the twentieth century to one million and more.

The House of Harper's led the way for mass circulation periodicals with the publication of *Harper's New Monthly Magazine* in 1850. It was conceived as a literary magazine with the primary focus of selling the books Harper's published. The high quality of both the writing and the wood engraved illustrations made *Harper's Monthly* successful enough to encourage a weekly publication, *Harper's Weekly*, in 1857. The weekly publication featured double-page, wood engraved political cartoons and subjects of current interest. Thomas Nast published his well-known political cartoons in *Harper's Weekly*, and Winslow Homer's Civil War illustrations were eagerly sought by families wanting pictures of their boys at battle.

Harper's branched out into specialty publications in 1867 with *Harper's Bazar*, a fashion magazine with articles and fiction written primarily for a female audience. *Harper's Young People*, a juvenile serial, started in 1863. The publisher's talented art department provided the drawings for the juvenile illustrations, introducing children to such illustrators as Frederic Remington and Howard Pyle.

As art editor, Charles Parsons discovered and nurtured the talents of many young illustrators who set the standards of quality and style for the generation to follow. Among these "old timers" were: Edwin Austin Abbey, Frederic Remington, William T. Smedley, Howard Pyle, Arthur Burdett Frost, Charles Reinhart, and A.R. Waud.

The only serious competitors for *Harper's Monthly* in terms of quality literary magazines were the *Atlantic Monthly*, which was not illustrated, and *Scribner's Magazine*. Josiah Gilbert Holland, Roswell Smith, and Charles Scribner published the first *Scribner's Monthly* in November of 1870. It was a general literary magazine with lavish and elegant illustrations. In 1881, disagreements between Charles Scribner's Sons, the book publishers; and Scribner & Company, the magazine

publisher; led to Scribner & Company selling the magazine to the Century Company. The name *Scribner's*, it was agreed, would not be used for the new publication, and in turn Scribner & Company was not to start another magazine with that name for five years. In 1887, a new *Scribner's Magazine* was issued. The recognizable yellow cover was designed by architect Standford White. Russell Strugis and Joseph Hawley Chapin were two of the art editors during the magazine's tenure. Frederick Yohn, Olive Rush, Frank Masters, Karl Anderson, Henry Hutt, Arthur Keller, Ernest Peixotto, Walter Appleton Clark, and Arthur Burdett Frost were among the illustrators for the new *Scribner's*. Around 1912, the popularity of the magazine declined, due partially to the advent of many other magazines which had more popular appeal. The quality of the magazine declined after World War One and ceased publication altogether in 1939.

The Century Company, which had acquired the original *Scribner's*, took the name *Century Magazine*, which was based on the popular Century Club in New York. Like its predecessor, it was a quality literary monthly. Alexander Drake was art editor. Like Parsons, he had a talent for finding artists who had great potential as illustrators. Timothy Cole worked in the engraving department and established a reputation as the finest wood engraver of the period. Theodore DeVinne, the printer, also set high standards in typography and printing. When the halftone process replaced wood engravings, Century Company changed to a rotary press which printed halftones from cylindrical plates. They provided the finest reproductions of any magazine. In the 1890s, illustrators such as E.B. Kemble, Jay Hambidge, André Castaigne, Arthur Burdett Frost, and Albert Sterner contributed drawings to the magazine. Frank Croninshield was art editor from 1910 to 1913. *Century* suffered the same fate as *Harper's* in that competition from cheaper, more popular magazines cut into its subscriptions. After 1919, there were fewer illustrations in the magazine, and by 1920, there were only line cuts.

The juvenile offshoot of *Scribner's* was the periodical, *St. Nicholas Magazine*. After the sale of *Scribner's*, *St. Nicholas Magazine* became part of the Century Company. The first issue was published in 1873, three years after the first issue of *Scribner's Monthly*. Mary Mapes Dodge, who had already established her reputation in children's literature as the author of *Hans Brinker*, was editor of the magazine. Although the prevalent attitude towards children's literature was that it should be moralizing and educational, Dodge believed that children should be entertained by their books. She also shattered the popular belief that children were unable to distinguish between quality and shoddy work. She demanded very high standards from both the authors and illustrators of *St. Nicholas Magazine*. Her beliefs paid off. At a subscription rate of three dollars a year, high in comparison to other periodicals, parents of her young readers eagerly bought the magazine. Many of the stories and illustrations that were first published in *St. Nicholas Magazine* became the most popular in American juvenile literature. Dodge died in 1905, but her standards were continued after her death. The juvenile serial ran until the 1940s.

cover design
Norman Mills Price • Cat. no. 118
(reproduced in colour on the cover)

If a periodical exclusively for children could survive, publishers realized that other selective audiences could be targeted as well. In 1874, two brothers in Cleveland, Ohio — S.L. and Frederick Thorpe — published a paper aimed at a female audience. In the beginning, it was basically a cheap advertising paper encouraging the mail order business. Then in 1878, the brothers bought *Little Ones at Home*, a juvenile periodical, and renamed the magazine *Home Companion: Monthly for Young People*. In 1881, the surviving brother Frederick sold that periodical to E.B. Harvey, who quickly sold it again to three men, John S. Crowell, T.J. Kirkpatrick, and Phineas Price Mast. The magazine went through other fluctuations in focus and title changes until, in 1886, it was called *Ladies' Home Companion*. The semi-monthly publication reached one hundred thousand subscribers in 1890, bringing them household hints, needlework patterns, recipes, and ideas for home decoration and fashion. It was issued monthly from 1896 and in 1897, a final name change made the magazine the *Women's Home Companion*. This helped to distinguish it from the popular *Ladies' Home Journal*. Subscriptions for the *Companion* in 1898 numbered three hundred thousand. Fiction was added as a regular feature and illustrators such as Lucius Hitchcock, Hanson Booth, Armand Both, Harry Linnell, and Walter De Maris contributed high quality drawings. Joseph P. Knapp purchased the magazine in 1906, and it had a strong following through World War One, the twenties, and the Depression. The final issue was published in January of 1957.

The Ladies' Home Journal and Practical Housekeeper was originally an insert serial for Cyrus Curtis' *Tribune & Farmer* paper. It was edited by his wife, who used the name Louisa Knapp. Its popularity encouraged Curtis to issue it as a separate magazine in 1884. By 1889, just short of a half-million subscription list, Mrs. Curtis quit the magazine. Her husband hired a young man, Edward Bok, in her place. Bok kept the tone set by Mrs. Curtis, and the periodical continued to grow in popularity. It featured articles on housekeeping, health, child rearing, and fancywork, along with some fiction. By 1903, the circulation reached one million — the first American periodical to do so. The periodical began changing covers on each issue and including four-colour plates. There were strict editorial policies against tobacco, gambling, or alcohol appearing in the illustrations. By 1919, the circulation was two million and growing. Bok stayed with the *Journal* until 1920. Many of the illustrations were photographs, but fiction and articles were illustrated by the top illustrators of the day such as:Arthur William Brown, Denman Fink, George Brehm, Ernest Fuhr, and Frank Snapp.

The Delineator was another early magazine for female readers. In 1863, Ebenezer Butterick of Fitchburg, Massachusetts began a business, selling fashion patterns printed on tissue paper. He built this novel idea into Butterick & Company, and in 1873 issued a publication offering wood engraved illustrations of his fashions. Women who subscribed to *The Delineator* could choose the fashions they liked and order the patterns from the company. In the late 1880s, men's fashions were added as well as sections on books and other topics of interest. In 1899, the magazine was re-organized completely, and fiction was added as a regular feature. At first, *The Delineator* attracted neither top-name authors nor illustrators, but as the popularity of the magazine grew, better fiction and illustrations were found in its pages. In 1907, Theodore Dreiser was made editor. Gone was the homespun tone of the early years. The periodical now featured articles on society, theatre, royalty, and high fashion. The best illustrators, such as Howard Chandler Christy, Henry Hutt, W.T. Benda, Herman Pfeifer, and Arthur Keller worked for the magazine.

The American Magazine was the name of another popular monthly. It started in 1876 as *Frank Leslie's Popular Monthly*. The magazine offered short stories, poetry, and essays on travel, science, and the arts. It was well illustrated with wood engravings and chromolithographs. Leslie's widow continued the periodical after her husband's death in 1880. In 1905, it was renamed the *American Illustrated Magazine* and then shortened merely to *The American Magazine*. In 1906, a disgruntled group of authors and editors from *McClure's* purchased the periodical and turned it into their vehicle for the popular muckraking style of articles published at the time. Muckrakers was a term applied to authors and journalists who exposed corruption in business and government in the United States. The movement lasted roughly from 1902 - 1917, and such magazines as *McClure's*, *The American Magazine*, *Collier's*, *Cosmopolitan*, *Everybody*, *The Masses* and the *New York World* led the way. By 1915, the popularity of *The American Magazine* had dropped. It was sold to Crowell Company which already published the *Woman's Home Companion*. The focus of the periodical turned to domestic life and family interests. Between 1906 and 1917, a few of the illustrators whose work appeared in *The American Magazine* were: Paul Stahr, Dan Groesbeck, W.E. Hill, Norman Price, Frank Schoonover, May Wilson Preston, Martin Justice, Rose O'Neill, Charles Sarka, George Harding, Jay Hambidge, Arthur Dove, Rollin Kirby, Charles Relyea, and James Preston.

Although humorous weeklies were popular in Europe from the mid-nineteenth century on, Americans had no such weekly until 1877. Joseph Keppler, a German immigrant, who had worked for *Leslie's Illustrated Newspaper*, formed a partnership with A. Schwarzmann to issue a humorous weekly in German called *Puck*. Sydney Rosenfeld saw the paper and thought an English version of the same paper would do well. He became the editor of the English version which featured cartoons satirizing politics, society, and prominent public figures. There were also fiction stories and reviews. In 1894, Keppler died and his son Joseph Keppler, Jr. took over. Artist-illustrators who made their names as satirists in the magazine included: John Cassel, Rose O'Neill, Frank Nankivell, Gordon Grant, Will Crawford, W.E. Hill, Stuart Travis, and May Wilson Preston. The covers featured humorous and clever designs. Early in their careers, Everett Shinn and John Marin contributed covers to *Puck*. In 1904, John Kenderick Bangs became editor. In 1917, it was sold to Hearst's International, but it failed to revive the magazine. September, 1918 was the last issue.

In October of 1881, a disagreement within the art department at *Puck* led a group of artists to break with the magazine and found their own humorous periodical, *Judge*. At first *Judge* was very much like *Puck*, which resulted in a problem finding its own audience. The magazine was sold and re-organized several times before it caught on as a popular humorous weekly. By the turn of the century, *Judge* had surpassed *Puck* in popularity and was competing with *Life* for subscribers.

John Ames Mitchell was working as an illustrator in New York in 1882 when he teamed up with Edward Sanford Martin to start a new humorous weekly. The publication, called *Life*, was a picture magazine. In the beginning nearly all the art work was done by Mitchell. The first few issues sold poorly, but eventually there were enough subscribers for the two men to introduce new writers and illustrators. By 1890, there were fifty thousand subscribers. Charles Dana Gibson introduced his "Gibson Girl" in 1889, and the public eagerly followed her and her handsome, square-jawed beau for the next twenty years in the pages of *Life*. Other illustrators included: Otto Toaspern, Albert Levering, Otto Lang, William L. Jacobs, James Montgomery Flagg, and Orson Lowell. Mitchell died in 1918, and in 1920, Charles Dana Gibson was persuaded by friends to buy the struggling magazine. His efforts to save the magazine failed and it subsequently merged with Time, Inc.

Outing began publishing in 1882, as a gentleman's magazine dedicated to recreation. William Bailey Howland of Albany, New York, was the founder. Soon after its first issue it merged with *Wheelman*, a popular bicycling magazine. Sporting activities such as hunting, yachting, fishing, travelling, and camping were profiled in its pages. It often used photographs as illustrations instead of drawings. Illustrators associated with *Outing* were: N.C. Wyeth, Charles Livingston Bull, and Frank Schoonover. By 1905, it had a circulation of one hundred thousand. April, 1923 was the last issue.

The Cosmopolitan Magazine was started by Paul J. Schlicht in 1886, as a general literary magazine which changed its focus many times. Its beginnings are uncertain because it was moved from Rochester to New York City and then was sold twice — the second time to John Brisben Walker. Under Walker, *Cosmopolitan* became one of the leading illustrated magazines of the 1890s. In 1905, it was sold to William Randolph Hearst, and by 1914, circulation had reached one million. *Cosmopolitan* was one of the leading muckrakers, but it outgrew that vogue as did the other muckrakers, and after 1912, its emphasis was on fiction, particularly adventures and mysteries. The cover featured "pretty girl" faces by Harrison Fisher for many years. Art editor, William C. Gibson, bought work from the best known illustrators of the day. In 1921, the title was changed to *Hearst's International*, but a merger in 1922 resulted in using the title *Cosmopolitan* on the cover. During the "Roaring Twenties" it featured the daring, racy illustrations of James Montgomery Flagg and John Held.

Peter Fenelon Collier, an Irish immigrant, began a weekly magazine in 1888, featuring current events as well as fiction, essays on arts and humanities, humorous yarns, and sports. For the news sections he relied on halftone photographs, but most of the fiction and essays were illustrated by drawings. By 1892, the subscription list had a quarter of a million names. Robert Collier, son of the founder, was put in charge of the magazine in 1898 and improved the quality of both the writing and illustrations. In a 1906 promotional advertisement, *Collier's* promised yearly subscribers colour covers by the best illustrators, fifty-two frontispieces in colour and double-page drawings with decorative borders in each issue. *Collier's* boasted exclusive contracts with the illustrators Albert Sterner and Walter Appleton Clark. It also included the finest work of Charles Dana Gibson, Frederic Remington, Jessie Willcox Smith, E.W. Kemble, W.T. Smedley, Arthur Burdett Frost, the Leyendecker brothers, Sarah S. Stilwell, Edward Penfield, Henry Reuterdahl, and Maxfield Parrish. Robert Collier died in 1918, just as the circulation reached more than one million. The magazine was sold shortly afterward and although it experienced difficulties, it was back in publication by 1920.

McClure's Magazine was the creation of Samuel Sidney

"The Deserter"
Will Crawford • Cat. no. 44

McClure who issued the first copy in June of 1893. Serialized articles on Napoleon, and then Lincoln, by Ida Tarbell won the recognition of the public, and the circulation began to grow. By 1896, there were a quarter-million readers. Auguste F. Jaccaci was *McClure's* art editor and secured the works of illustrators: James and May Wilson Preston, Peter Newell, Thornton Skidmore, W.T. Benda, Lucius Hitchcock, William Oberhardt, Wallace Morgan, Arthur Keller, Edmund Ashe, Alice Barber Stephens, and Armand Both. One interesting feature of the periodical was the inclusion of small inset pictures of authors and illustrators in the title next to their names. Circulation was strong until the 1920s when *McClure's* popularity tapered off.

To place the *Saturday Evening Post* in a chronology of American magazines is difficult. Its publishers in the twentieth century claimed a direct link to Benjamin Franklin's *Pennsylvania Gazette* of 1728. Throughout most of the nineteenth century, the *Post* was a cheap story magazine with little prestige. It was owned at different times by a variety of publishers. Cyrus Curtis, who published the *Ladies' Home Journal,* bought the title and a subscription list of two thousand in 1897. Banking on the popularity of its long-standing name, Curtis re-organized the periodical into a bestseller. George Horace Lorimer was made editor in 1899, and Curtis honoured Lorimer's desire to make the *Post* a men's magazine, a complement to the *Journal.* Articles featured business success stories, community affairs, current events, and fiction with themes of adventure and romance. From the beginning of Curtis' involvement with the *Post,* the magazine was a success with circulation at half a million by 1903, and two million by 1913.

Before 1912, the covers were a familiar black and orange, usually featuring one of the popular "pretty girl" faces. But after 1912, the magazine published covers with themes of American life. Norman Rockwell published his first cover with the *Post* in 1916, and was a popular contributor through to the 1960s. The *Post* maintained its popularity by celebrating the prosperous, conservative spirit of American life.

Success Magazine did not enjoy the longevity of other periodicals of the time. In its short tenure, 1897 to 1911, it attracted many good writers and the best of the popular illustrators. Orison Sweet Marden and Louis Klopsch were partners in this publication, which focused on fiction and non-fiction stories of successful people. In 1911, it had three hundred thousand subscribers when it was abandoned. It was re-issued again in 1918 as the *New Success.* The publication never achieved its namesake's popularity and was discontinued shortly thereafter.

Everybody's Magazine was another title that did not survive many years. Originally it was founded by John Wanamaker, a Philadelphia merchant. It ran from 1899 to 1929, and featured both news events and fiction. It was also active in the muckraking movement until 1914. Illustrators found in the pages of *Everybody's* included: Frederick Richardson, Anna Whelan Betts, Karl Anderson, George Wright, Albert Wenzell, Percy Cowen, W.E. Hill, Robert Edwards, and Will Crawford.

NOTES

1. Frank Luther Mott, *A History of American Magazines, 1885-1905,* vol. 4 (Cambridge, 1957), p. 11.

THE BOOKS

Although magazines provided most assignments for illustrators between 1890 and 1920, there were also many hardcover books published that required illustrations. The reading public in America during this period had a definite preference for fiction. Publishers of hardcover fiction were only one step ahead of the public demand for more books to read. Before 1890, selling one hundred thousand copies of a hardcover book was considered a great success. But after 1890, a bestseller could run into the hundreds of thousands. In some exceptional cases, like Eleanor Porter's *Pollyanna* (1913), more than one million copies were sold.

 THE PIRATE
HELENA SHARPSTEEN

"I want to be a pirate / And sail upon the sea /..."
Blanche V. Fisher • Cat. no. 56

47

Magazines were largely responsible for this surge in novel reading. Readers had had a steady diet of fiction in their magazines, and this whetted their appetites for more. Also, many magazine stories that had been serialized over a number of months were reprinted as hardcover books. An editor at Estes & Lauriat stated that it was: "impossible to make the books of most American authors pay unless they are first published and acquire recognition through the columns of the magazines."[1] Usually one or more of the illustrations from the magazine serial were used in the book, but only occasionally did the illustrator receive a royalty from the book sales.

There were many publishers of hardcover, illustrated fiction. A few were also publishers of magazines; others sought reprint rights from magazines. They also solicited manuscripts from authors made famous by magazines. New York was the centre of book publishing, with the

biggest publishers being the House of Harper, Appleton & Company, Charles Scribner's Sons, Century Company, Doubleday & Company, Grosset & Dunlap, and Dodd, Mead & Company. In Boston there were Houghton Mifflin and L.C. Page & Company. J.B. Lippincott & Company was headquartered in Philadelphia, and Stone & Kimball in Chicago.

The main difference between book and periodical illustration was the time factor. Book publishers had the benefit of several months to prepare for publication. Authors were shown the illustrations before publication so that changes could be made. Relationships between authors and illustrators varied. Authors Julian Hawthorne and Edith Wharton, for example, both opposed illustrations in their books, but many were illustrated in spite of their protests.

Most publishers believed that illustrations were a key factor in selling books. There is evidence that the

"I do n't think, looking it over, I did the wrong thing…"
Arthur William Brown • Cat. no. 26

publishers were right. For example, the illustrations that Frederick Yohn did for John Fox's *The Lone Pine Trail* (1908), were so popular that the publishers were deluged with requests for reprints of the pictures. They also received several inquiries about whether or not the originals were for sale. Ideally, the relationship between author and illustrator was that of a team. Illustrator Arthur William Brown reminisced about his early years in illustrating:

> [Illustrators] enjoyed a certain prestige and dignity seldom found today. Illustrator and author often teamed up to talk over picture situations and continued to collaborate, sometimes for years.[2]

Authors, however, were often hesitant in trusting illustrations for fear the public might misunderstand a character or setting should the illustrator's interpretation not match the author's intentions. Mark Twain expressed his concern with mild sarcasm to illustrator Dan Beard on the prospect of the latter illustrating *A Connecticut Yankee in King Arthur's Court* (1889):

> Mr. Beard," he said, with a drawl, "I don't want to subject you to any undue suffering, but I wish you would read the book before you illustrate it.[3]

Stephen Backspace, most likely a pen-name for the unidentified author, was equally sarcastic in his "appreciation" of the drawings the illustrator Straboni had done for his novel *Priscilla's Hectic Past* (1919). He wrote to the publisher:

> The pictures for my novel... go back to you today by mail. Thanks for the opportunity of viewing them... in looking over the pictures it has occured to me that perhaps one or two alterations in the text would be advisable... on page 6, second paragraph: "Gerald Fusilage paced thoughtfully to the heavily-draped window and gazed out upon the restless afternoon activity of the Avenue. He was well over average height and carried himself with the assured erectness of the trained soldier that he was. Standing there before the long casement, with the pale winter sunlight outlining his well-knit form, he presented a fine picture of a masculine beauty..." This should be corrected to read: "Gerald Fusilage slumped into a kitchen chair and fixed his gaze dejectedly on a pandanus standing in an oddly-fashioned *Jardiniere* just inside the doorway. He was rather under the average height and stooped with the studious stoopiness of the student that he was. Sitting there before the small open win-

dow, with its charmingly simple sash-curtain of dotted muslin, the radiant summer sunlight splashing the linoleum at his feet, he presented a striking example of a better-class burglar, and even the well-cut uniform of the New York Cleaning Service that he wore failed to disguise his criminality, etc. ... On page 65, last paragraph... "From the coiled masses of her coppery hair to the last inch of her jewel-bedecked slipper she was queenliness itself. A white gown of severe simplicity followed the lithe grace of her perfect form, etc." This should read: *"Fat* was the first word that came to Gerald as he glanced lazily up at her. From the top of her rubber swimming cap to the tip of her black-stockinged toe she was pudginess itself. A one-piece bathing suit of some closely clinging material was slightly in advance of the generous rotundity of her perfect amplitude, etc."... Trusting that you may agree with me as to the advisability of correcting the text of the novel to accord more delicately with the conceptions of the artist,...[4]

It was not uncommon for publishers to ask authors to change the text to suit the illustrations. Backspace humorously directed this letter as a protest against what he considered an inane practice.

The publishing of hardcover books opened up several opportunities for artists beyond the illustrations themselves. In addition to brightly coloured, full-cloth bindings, the covers were often adorned with four-colour halftone reproductions glued to the face. Endpapers were specially designed to fit the themes in the novels. Poster designs were also needed to advertise the books. Sometimes promotional gimmicks involved the illustrator designing a special display which could fit into the windows of booksellers across America. Book publishing was a booming business in this era. It provided a showcase not only for the talents of new American authors, but for the artist-illustrators as well.

NOTES

1. Frank Luther Mott, *A History of American Magazines, 1885-1905,* vol. 4 (Cambridge, 1957), p. 41.
2. Arthur William Brown, "The decade: 1910-1920", *The Illustrator in America 1900-1960's,* compiled and edited by Walt Reed, (New York, 1966), p. 43.
3. *Success Magazine,* (April, 1905), p. 299.
4. [Letter to the editor], *The Bookman,* vol. 49 (1919), pp. 43-44.

THE ILLUSTRATIONS

he subjects of illustrations reflect the diversity of interests and the wide variety of reading materials available to the public during this era. The following essays divide those subjects into twelve groupings. The first four essays deal with American society — the upper classes, the masses, the family, and the country folk. This is followed by five essays that treat literary genres — romance, adventure, suspense, animal and children's stories. Finally, topical issues of the era are covered in three remaining sections — war, sports, and travel.

These short essays are intended as brief discussions on topics in American book and periodical illustration. Although introductory in approach, they will hopefully raise issues and questions which can be studied further through in-depth research using the Glenbow Museum illustration collection and similar collections elsewhere. Historians use many materials and methods to better interpret the past. To know what people read and to see the pictures which enhanced that reading material is to gain a unique entrée into the minds and attitudes of Americans living in those decades flanking the turn of the twentieth century.

"St. Lawrence River"
William James Aylward • Cat. no. 5

"Dutch sat down and fanned himself with his hat..."
Charles Nicolas Sarka • Cat. no. 126

"Nothing is to be heard except the low swish of branches"
Charles Livingston Bull • Cat. no. 30

[Boys fleeing], cover design
Herman Pfeifer • Cat. no. 112

"Autumn"
Clara Elsene Peck • Cat. no. 108

"Building the lynx cabane"
Frank Earle Schoonover • Cat. no. 129

[Fox chasing cardinal]
Charles Livingston Bull • Cat. no. 31

[Luncheon]
Charles M. Relyea • Cat. no. 121

THE SMART SET

The girl being a beauty, all the rest was easy enough. I gave her theatre party after theatre party, followed by charming little suppers, asked to them the jeunesse dorée of the day; took her repeatedly to the opera, and saw that she was there always surrounded by admirers; incessantly talked of her fascinations; assured my young friends that she was endowed with a fortune equal to the mines of Ophir, that she danced like a dream, and possessed all the graces, a sunbeam across one's path...

Samuel Ward McAllister, *Society as I Have Found It*

[In a theatre box]
William Ely Hill • Cat. no. 79

he "Smart Set" in America comprised families which had won great fortunes in railroads, oil, mining, and other industries fundamental to the growing modern economy following the U.S. Civil War. They lived, for the most part, in New York City and summered at the resort towns of Newport, Lenox and Bar Harbor. It was not money alone that gave one entrée into high society. Many newly rich families from the West and Midwest came to New York only to find themselves snubbed. Samuel Ward McAllister was considered the arbiter of New York and Newport society. When Mrs. Astor, the patroness of New York's social register, wanted to give a fancy ball, it was McAllister she turned to for advice on the guest list. As her ballroom would only hold four hundred comfortably, the guest list was restricted to that number. It was from that guest list that the term "the 400" was coined, and thus began the great struggle to be "in the 400."

But if one was out of "the 400," there were plenty of opportunities for observing those who were in. Newspapers and magazines in the 1890s illustrated the elites' every move — a walk up Fifth Avenue, polo at Prospect Park, an evening at Delmonico's, croquet on the front lawn of a mansion, or a pony ride in Newport. The parties of the smart set were lavish to the point of opulence. It was a time of conspicuous consumption.

"She became aware — with a sudden mortification,
of her over elaborate appearance."
Harry Spafford Potter • Cat. no. 114

Double-page illustrations in popular magazines featured the weddings of American society girls to titled European men. Reporters and artists were sent to cover the balls for an eager public, waiting to know what the guests wore and learn about the extravaganzas the host and hostess had dreamed up. One host ordered nightingales in rose trees to serenade the guests. Another had an elaborate stage constructed at his home so a Broadway play could be performed as after-dinner entertainment.

Town Topics and *The Smart Set* were the periodicals of high society that focused on gossip about the very rich. Neither was particularly well illustrated. Although intended exclusively for high society, both magazines were usually purchased and read by those who only dreamed of belonging.

High society had many illustrators, few of whom became wealthy enough to be part of the society they painted. Arthur Keller, Charles Dana Gibson, Howard Chandler Christy, Albert Wenzell, Henry Hutt, James Montgomery Flagg, Harrison Fisher, and the Leyendecker brothers, Joseph and Frank, all rendered the glamorous women and their handsome escorts in the pages of the popular magazine.

There was also a vogue for romance stories and novels involving the very rich. George Barr McCutcheon and Paul Leister Ford were masters of this genre. McCutcheon's *Day of the Dog* (1905), illustrated by Harrison Fisher, and Ford's *Wanted - A Chaperon* (1902), illustrated by Howard Chandler Christy, are examples of these short love stories. The books were usually novelettes, which could be read in one sitting, and were elaborately designed with embossed bindings, decorated pages, and illustrated by the best society illustrators. They were marketed as gift books, and made a perfect present for a gentleman to give a lady.

The "Gay Nineties" was the era of genteel society. Certainly the very wealthy continued with their parties and outings into the twentieth century, but the rest of American society turned its attention elsewhere. *Life* and *Puck* published satirical cartoons aimed at high society and the muckrakers pointed the finger at wealthy businessmen whom they blamed for corruption and vice. New social awareness made the contrast between poor and wealthy even more painfully evident. And the realists in fiction began to write about the empty lives of monied snobs and petted debutantes.

William Dean Howells was one of the authors to take an interest in the social and economic problems of his era. In *Hazard of New Fortunes* (1890), he looked at New York society, contrasting the offensive personalities of two debutantes trying to break into society, with the personality of their mild, gentle-mannered brother. The book was illustrated by W.A. Rogers, a noted political cartoonist. Rogers' line drawings matched the penetrating truthfulness of the story.

Lily Bart was the heroine of Edith Wharton's *House of Mirth* (1905). She had social connections and beauty, but little money, and desperately needed to make a good marriage. She failed, was snubbed by her "friends," and took her own life in the end. Wharton's novel was a thoughtful study of the tragedies and ironies of New York society, yet the publishers picked Albert Wenzell as an illustrator who was no counterpart to the author's seriousness. Wenzell, although an excellent draftsman, dealt with the playful, trifling aspects of society, and his illustrations seem inappropriate to the tragic story.

Booth Tarkington's *The Magnificent Ambersons* (1918), examined the life and attitudes of a young man, not from New York society, but from "Midland town." This arrogant son of a wealthy family, was scornful of his Midwestern neighbours. In the end the young man developed a more positive attitude. Arthur William Brown sensitively portrayed this story in his illustrations. Tarkington's earlier novel *Seventeen* (1916), was illustrated by Brown as well — an indication that the author was pleased with Brown's pictorial interpretations of his stories.

The decade following World War One ushered many changes into American society. H.L. Mencken called the short-skirted, bobbed-hair girls the "flappers," and John Held drew pages of them for *Vanity Fair, Life, Cosmopolitan,* and *The New Yorker.* Oliver Herford illustrated a satirical *Deb's Dictionary* to help the uninitiated understand the new age. He summed up the "Roaring Twenties" with these few examples:

"Belle" — A Deb who never goes to bed the same day she gets up; "Ear" — A once-admired feminine feature, driven into obscurity by the sensational debut of the KNEE as a popular favourite; "Jilt" — A Deb who refuses to take on more than one Fiancé at a time; "Vulgar" — The kind of people who are getting everywhere nowadays.

The society pages after World War One no longer concentrated on a few wealthy people from the "right" families. Instead the public wanted stories and pictures of movie stars and radio personalities. Magazines also featured the fast-paced life of the young crowd who frequented jazz clubs, danced the Charleston and drank bootleg gin. The "Roaring Twenties" was an explosive release from the restrictive, prim and proper generations of the "Gay Nineties."

THE MASSES

o me it seemed that all the spirit of rural America, its idealism, its dreams, the passion of a Brown, the courage and patience and sadness of a Lincoln, the dreams and courage of a Lee or a Jackson were all here. The very soil smacked of American idealism and faith, a fixedness in sentimental and purely imaginative American tradition in which I, alas, could not share — I had seen Pittsburgh.

Theodore Dreiser

Do illustration for a while. It won't hurt you. Go into the streets and look at life.

John Sloan

"The Village About the Towering Chimneys"
Charlotte Harding • Cat. no. 75

n sharp contrast to the opulent manners of high society at the turn of the century in America, masses of city dwellers barely eked out the means to survive. Immigrants who had heard the streets of America were paved with gold, poured into the United States between 1890 and 1920, from countries such as Italy, Germany, Poland, Ireland, Sweden, Norway, Russia, and Japan. Many headed for the Midwest seeking farm land, but found work in factories instead, competing for jobs with poor, working class Americans. All over America this great influx of new people was creating larger cities. And cities were unprepared for such rapid growth. In New York, immigrants moved into neighbourhoods where their language was spoken and customs retained. But housing was inadequate to accommodate so many people, and low-paying jobs prevented many immigrants from improving their conditions. In 1900, more than two million children under fifteen worked in factories to help

"The Registry Desk, Ellis Island"
Gerald W. Peters • Cat. no. 111

support their families. Sweatshops paid ten dollars a week or five hundred and twenty dollars a year. Tenement life came to mean overcrowded buildings which were filthy and unsafe. Fires swept through neighbourhoods killing some residents and leaving others homeless. Landlords charged immigrants high rents; laws to protect these newcomers were practically non-existent, and government social programs were inefficient.

Gerald W. Peters was an illustrator particularly attracted to immigrants. He illustrated an article in 1903 for Jacob A. Riis published by *Century* called "The Hyphenated American" (cat. no. 111). So sensitive and expressive were his drawings that they were published again, thirteen years later as a pictorial essay on immigrants. Writings like those by Riis, using illustrations and photographs of the squalid conditions of tenement living, slowly brought about changes in the laws.

Another sharp contrast existed in the literature of the period. While the public enjoyed lighthearted romances, historical fiction, and Western novels, they also read literature that supported both the progressive and muckraking movements. Such literature sought to improve the lives of working class people and raise the moral standards of business.

Theodore Dreiser wrote *Sister Carrie* (1900), a novel considered by many to be a scandalous picture of the corruption of a young woman subjected to city life. Frank Norris laid bare the corruption and malpractice in the transportation of wheat by the Pacific and Southwest Railway in his novel *The Octopus* (1901). Upton Sinclair portrayed the sombre lives of those associated with the Chicago stockyards in his book *The Jungle* (1906).

William Sydney Porter, better known as O. Henry, wrote about the mundane lives of common people in big cities. Collections of his stories are: *Cabbages and Kings* (1904), *The Four Million* (1906), *The Voice of the City* (1908), *Strictly Business* (1910), and *Waifs and Strays* (1917). Illustrators who teamed with O. Henry included: James Preston, Will Crawford, Gordon Grant, Frank Verbeck, James Montgomery Flagg, and F. Luis Mora.

The semi-realism of authors such as O. Henry and Booth Tarkington, and the naturalism of authors such as Jack London, Stephen Crane, and Hamlin Garland, demanded a new type of illustration. Four Philadelphians, George Luks, John Sloan, William Glackens, and Everett Shinn were among the artists who formed a group called "The Eight." They began as newspaper artists, and were trained to portray human society as objectively and truthfully as possible. Because newspaper artists had to work quickly, they evolved a

brisk, simple style of drawing which was reinforced through their common teacher, Robert Henri. There was a frankness and veracity to their drawings which complemented the writers of the new realism.

Luks, Sloan, Glackens, and Shinn admired the work of Abbey and Pyle, but complained that these American illustrators dealt with historical subjects; therefore, they had little in common with them. Instead, they studied the works of English illustrators and artists such as Hogarth, Cruikshank, and Leech, and French artists such as Steinlin and Forain. These European illustrators drew their subjects from life with such credibility that they were often accused of vulgarity. The American artists shared the desire to break with the formalized studio painting techniques and the bathos and melodrama of other magazine illustrators. Sloan encouraged his students and artist friends to do illustration before embarking on a career as a fine artist. He argued that it was excellent training to go to the streets, bar rooms, flophouses, and the tenements to observe first hand the people and their lives. To a public audience accustomed to the lush, finished drawings of Hutt or Fisher, these artists seemed coarse and unrefined. Critics dubbed the group "The Revolutionary Black Gang," "The Apostles of Ugliness," and the "Ash Can School."

As newspaper artists were replaced by photographers, many Philadelphia illustrators headed for New York to find work with magazines. Periodical illustrations reached a far greater audience, and soon the influence of "The Eight" was felt on a national scale.

Ernest Fuhr, a newspaper artist for the *New York World* and the *New York Herald*, was one of the first to be influenced by the Philadelphian artists. He became friends with Sloan, Glackens, and Henri, and although Fuhr's subjects were more varied than theirs, he used the same realistic and quick style in his work. The illustrator Frederico Gruger, had been associated with Luks, Sloan, Glackens, and Shinn in Philadelphia as a member of The Charcoal Club. His illustrations reflect the same lively, agile quality. James Preston had also been a member of The Charcoal Club, and was influenced by Henri and Sloan.

There were two women also associated with what came to be called the Philadelphia School. Both were married to illustrators. May Wilson Preston married James Preston in 1903. She was already a recognized illustrator at the time of her marriage. Her illustrations are taken from direct observation of city life. They reflect her good sense of humour. Often her subjects were caught in the comic acts of everyday events. Mrs. Preston worked from models, sketches, and an enormous file of pictures, which she diligently collected. She

"The Colliery Huns returning home from work"
Thornton Oakley • Cat. no. 103

frequently visited the New York Public Library to find just the right detail for a setting she needed on a particular assignment. Florence Scovel Shinn was the first wife of Everett Shinn. Although she never achieved the renown of May Wilson Preston, she did enjoy popularity as the illustrator of Alice Hegan Rice's novels.

Wallace Morgan also practiced the realistic style, although he was not an intimate of the group. Morgan began his career as a newspaper artist and found that a quicker, more realistic style was a necessity. He always had a sketchbook with him to record faces and scenes. But when it came to commissioned illustrations, Morgan worked neither from sketches nor models. He was one of the few illustrators who worked directly from observation and memory. Morgan was an active illustrator through the 1930s and pictured high society as frequently as he pictured street life. Henry Patrick Raleigh also brought the newspaper style of drawing to a variety of subjects. Both Morgan and Raleigh worked quickly and during their careers completed hundreds of illustrating assignments.

The Masses was a weekly magazine, which began publishing in New York in 1912, and was dedicated to the plight of the working class in America. It supported a liberal, socialist point of view. Max Eastman was the editor, and he was very opinionated about the style and subjects of illustrations he wanted in the magazine. He wrote an article called "Journalism Versus Art" in which he stated:

> This, then, is the diagnosis of published art in America. It is business art. It does not aim to achieve the beautiful, the real, the ideal, the characteristic, the perfect, the sublimes, the ugly, the grotesque, the harmonious, the symetrical, or any other of those ends that various schools of art and art criticism have with similar merit set before them. It aims to achieve profits in competition. And any or all of those genuinely artistic aims are subordinated to that.[1]

Eastman published illustrators who expressed individualism in their drawings. Art Young, Maurice Becker, Robert Minor, Stuart Davis, and Charles A. Winter were but a handful of illustrators who contributed to this spirited periodical. There is a modernity to their work evidenced by the simplicity of style, expressiveness of line, and honesty in approach to the subjects.

Thornton Oakley was an illustrator who chose his subject matter from the industrialization of America. He visited shipyards, factories, coal mines, and lumberyards, and left a record of America's blue collar workers. In contrast to the penetrating candor of the Philadelphian artists, the power of Oakley's drawings came from their unusual compositions. As a student of Howard Pyle, Oakley learned to add drama and intensity to his works through design elements. Railway tracks spill into the reader's space, a ship's bow is rendered from a head-on point of view, a coal miner, off shift, walks down a path which leads straight forward, out of the picture plane (cat. no. 103). Unusual perspectives like these added energy to Oakley's portrayal of the working classes. As part of the World War One effort, Oakley contributed poster designs celebrating American industry.

Geritt A. Béneker, like Oakley, also sympathetically rendered images of American industrial workers. As a poet, artist, writer, Béneker believed that the best means of communication between labour and management was through the arts. He lived and worked at the Hydraulic Pressed Steel Company, drawing the people and work scenes he witnessed every day. He organized an exhibition comprising the paintings he had done following this experience. It toured the United States for many years. He lectured widely on his theories of art and labour. Many of his book and periodical illustrations focused on the theme of the working man. Béneker sold several of his illustrations to *Success Magazine*, a periodical which emphasized the portrayal of blue collar workers (cat. no. 11).

Many of the authors who wrote in a realistic style and uncovered the malignance and vice of American society, chose not to illustrate their books. During their heyday, illustrated books and periodicals carried a tone of frivolity that was opposite to these authors' purposes. They wanted the verbal descriptions in their texts to carry the reader's attention; illustrations would, they believed, dilute the potency of the written word. As authors turned their attention to the lower strata of society, describing life with a detached and objective narration, the need for illustrations disappeared.

NOTES

1. Max Eastman, *Journalism Versus Art*, (New York, n.d.), p. 23.

THE DOMESTIC SCENE

 would watch and study [children], and try to get them to take unconsciously the positions that I happened to be wanting for a picture. All the models I have ever had for my illustrations are just the adorable children of my kind friends, who would lend them to me for a little while. Such a thing as a paid model is an abomination and a travesty on childhood...

Jessie Willcox Smith, *Good Housekeeping*, (Oct., 1917)

[Grandmother and baby]
Alice Beach Winter • Cat. no. 147

uring the years 1890 to 1925 some important social changes were evolving in America. Not surprisingly, these changes touched on the family. Foremost was the Women's Rights Movement which had been born out of a reaction to the Industrial Revolution. The Women's Movement focused on many issues of women's rights including occupations, education, morality, and religion. With immigrants coming into the United States in large numbers and farm land in the Midwest already claimed, new generations born in America were having to push further west or move into the cities to take factory jobs. Traditional family life was then threatened by separation or by overcrowded competitive life in the cities.

Amidst all these changes, the home, motherhood, and family ties consistently appeared as dominant themes in popular literature. "Home and religion" stories were top-sellers in women's magazines. The family life portrayed in popular women's periodicals rarely addressed the radical changes in the status of the family at the turn of the century. The illustrations promoted values designed to maintain continuity with an idea of pre-industrial life in which everything was ordered or understandable. Women as managers of domestic life were advised on how to maintain a clean and efficient home, raise healthy, sweet-natured children, and maintain religious and moral values in the family.

The quality of life for women and children in middle and upper class families improved dramatically in the 1890s. New appliances in the home coupled with the low costs of hiring domestic help, gave American women more free time to read, and because of increasing prosperity, they also had money to spend on themselves and their families. That fact was not overlooked by advertisers and publishers.

The first magazine geared specifically towards women was *Ladies' Magazine* published in Boston. In 1837, Louis Antoine Godey bought the magazine and merged it with another he already owned, entitled *Lady's Book*. The new publication was called *Godey's Lady's Book*. *Godey's* was issued until 1898.

Because of *Godey's* success, other publishers saw women readers as an important audience. By the turn of the century the most widely read periodicals for women were *Ladies' Home Journal* and *Women's Home Companion*. The *Ladies' Home Journal* relied heavily on photographs to illustrate articles, but drawings by well-known illustrators were sprinkled throughout its pages. The magazine's changing cover was an added incentive for buying a new magazine each month, and other popular periodicals followed the *Journal's* lead. The

Woman's Home Companion was similar to the *Journal*, although not as elegant in design. It, too, relied heavily on photographs and ran articles on housekeeping, handiwork, gardening, menu planning, child rearing, party decoration, and other domestic concerns. Fiction in the *Companion* was supplied by such authors as Sherwood Anderson, Booth Tarkington, Sinclair Lewis, Margaret Deland, and Willa Cather. The illustrations came from equally reputable illustrators such as Lucius Hitchcock, Hanson Booth, Harry Linnell, and Walter De Maris.

Both the *Journal* and the *Companion* ran advertisements for household products. Because women had become chief consumers for the home and were more likely to purchase products, the artwork in the ads had to compete for their attention; therefore, it had to match the quality of the illustration. There was no stigma attached to illustrating for commercial purposes. Nearly all the leading illustrators of the day gladly illustrated for companies such as: Cream of Wheat, Campbell's Soup, Armour Beef Extract, Proctor and Gamble, National Biscuit Company, Ralston Purina, Colgate Company, Sunkist, Kodak, and Bon Ami. In the early decades of magazine advertisements, the sales pages were grouped together either at the beginning or the end of the periodical. Women's magazines were among the first to integrate advertisements into the body of the magazine.

American companies were eager to project wholesome, healthy images of the American family in their advertisements. Periodicals had strict guidelines for the illustrators to follow. Neither the *Journal* nor the *Companion* allowed references to alcohol in the illustrations. Any material deemed risque was sent back to the illustrator to be reworked. Likewise, publishers of women's magazines perpetuated the ideal of the American housewife and mother. For example, when Jessie Willcox Smith published a drawing of a sweet-faced girl in a pink dress digging seashells in the sand, letters came from mothers wanting to know where the illustrator had seen their daughters. This is exactly the response the art editor wanted. If a woman identified with the magazine she was likely to keep up her subscription.

Literature that focused on the family reflected innocence and sentimentality. Eleanor Porter's *Pollyanna* (1913), illustrated by Stockton Mulford, featured a young heroine whose optimistic "glad game" won the hearts of her bitter aunt and the whole town. It was a bestseller in the United States, and the word "Pollyanna," meaning any persistently optimistic person, entered into the dictionary. Kathleen Thompson Norris wrote numerous sentimental domestic novels, her bestseller being *Mother*

"This is the mother my father gave me long ago."
Alice Barber Stephens • Cat. no. 136

(1911), illustrated by Frederick Yohn. Alice Caldwell Hegan published a successful novel, *Mrs. Wiggs of the Cabbage Patch* (1901), about a social worker in Louisville. The illustrations were by Florence Scovel Shinn. Although sentimental in subject matter, Shinn's illustrations had a simple but expressive linear style that added greatly to the appeal of the book. Elizabeth Shippen Green supplied the tender illustrations for Annie Hamilton Donnell's *Rebecca Mary* (1905), with a colour cover, frontispiece and eight black and white illustrations. Alice Barber Stephens was another popular illustrator of family stories, illustrating the works of such authors as Mary E. Wilkins, Margaret Deland, Grace Richmond, and Olivia Howard Dunbar.

[Mother kissing her children good-bye]
Harry A. Linnell • Cat. no. 94

A welcome relief to the sentimental family novel came from author, Booth Tarkington. He began his career as an illustrator but switched to writing when, in 1895, he wrote and illustrated a satirical piece for *Life*. He humorously admitted: "Life paid me twenty dollars for this, mentioning that it paid thirteen dollars for the text and seven dollars for drawing. This helped me decide upon writing rather than illustrating as a career."[1] *Penrod* (1914), introduced Tarkington's most memorable character. This twelve-year-old boy had a very active imagination which constantly got him into one predicament after another; appropriately, the publishers looked outside the group of decorative, sentimental illustrators for an artist to do the illustrations. Gordon Grant, a cartoonist for *Life* and *Puck* (cat. no. 67), was selected. His sense of humour combined with a warmly realistic style, pleasingly complemented the text. *Penrod and Sam* (1916), was illustrated by Worth Brehm who gave the character Penrod both the puckish side of a rascal and the charm of a boy growing up. Willie Baxter from *Seventeen* (1916), was another memorable Tarkington character. Illustrator Arthur William Brown aptly pictured the pain and happiness of Willie as he finds romance with Lola.

Another break from images of the nostalgic family life came from the illustrator Rose O'Neill. She created the "Kewpies," chubby babies who were little mischief-makers. When the "Kewpies" appeared in the pages of *Ladies' Home Journal* and *Women's Home Companion*, they spawned a fad. "Kewpie" dolls were available along with other collectibles. O'Neill was also known for her images of Black Americans as seen in the cartoons she submitted to *Puck* (cat. no. 105). She treated her subjects with candour and humour. Although her social satires never intentionally degraded Afro-Americans, she was one of many illustrators of the period who perpetuated negative stereotypes of Blacks.

The American family of the sentimental novel was middle to upper class, affluent, Christian, and Caucasian. Yet at this time in history immigrants from all over the world were flocking to Ellis Island. Perhaps it was these "threats" from foreign influence affecting the American family unit that perpetrated the nostalgic images of domestic life.

Other threats to the family were expanding industrialization and growing cities which lured young people away from rural life. Hamlin Garland describes these threats in his autobiography *Son of the Middle Border* (1914):

> All about me as I traveled, I now perceived the mournful side of American "enterprise." Sons were deserting their work-worn fathers, daughters were forgetting their tired mothers. Families were everywhere breaking up. Ambitious young men and unsuccessful old men were in restless motion, spreading, swarming, dragging their reluctant women and their helpless and wondering children into unfamiliar hardships...

But these were trends that magazines generally ignored. When the Philadelphia Realists portrayed family life in slums or immigrant groups celebrating holidays foreign to Americans, the critics accused the artists of seeking out the ugly side of America. Magazines catered to the popular images in America at this time. The image of the American family in periodicals projected sentiments of security and happiness. Olive Rush's pictorial essay "Preparing Christmas Plum Pudding" for *Success* in 1903 (cat. no. 125), showed the whole family in the kitchen, pitching in to prepare the food for a traditional Christmas dinner. This, and so many images like it, spoke of prosperity and security in a country that was outgrowing its age of innocence.

NOTES

1. *An Exhibition of Booth Tarkington's Works*, Princeton University, (1946), p.7.

TOWN AND COUNTRY

 y hope now was to possess a minute isle of safety in the midst of the streaming currents of Western life — a little solid ground in my native valley on which surviving members of my family could catch and cling.

Hamlin Garland, *Son of the Middle Border*

"If some wood-chopping clown / should come from the town..."
James Moore Preston • Cat. no. 115

At the turn of the century much attention was focused on the rise of metropolitan cities, which lured farmers' children from the rural areas of America with promises of glamorous, successful careers. Yet, for those who had left rural or semi-rural areas and moved to the cities, there was a nostalgia for the simpler life of one's childhood. Writers who looked back included: Thomas Nelson Page in *In Ole Virginia* (1896), illustrated by Charles S. Reinhart; and Frank Stockton in *Rudder Grange* (1885), and *Pomona's Travels* (1894), both illustrated by Arthur Burdett Frost. Frost was at his best when drawing rustic country settings. However, he is best remembered for his drawings for Joel Chandler Harris' *Uncle Remus; His Songs and His Sayings* (1895). Harris wrote these tales based on stories Black neighbours had told him as a boy. Frederick Church illustrated the first book of *Uncle*

" 'Little Merry Smith,' he said, 'you're a wonder!' "
Gerald Leake • Cat. no. 92

Remus stories, but Harris was not satisfied with his drawings because they were too delicate and mild. Frost was asked to illustrate the second edition of the book and Harris was so pleased with the spirit, tone, and humour of these new drawings that he dedicated the book to the illustrator. Frost specialized in drawing country life in America, and *Collier's, Harper's, Century,* and *St. Nicholas Magazine* regularly featured his work. He also was well known as a sporting artist and published two books of his drawings — *Shooting Pictures* (1895), and *Sports and Games in the Open* (1899).

"Country life" pictures were a type of popular image much the same as the "he and she" or "pretty girl" picture. Examples of "country life" included: folks shopping in a country store, sons helping their fathers with chores, the minister greeting parishioners after church services, and the wholesome, pretty young girl walking down a country lane were all images portraying ideal American life. No illustrator did these drawings better than Norman Rockwell. He began his career in 1916 when he published his first cover for the *Saturday Evening Post* and continued to supply the *Post* with illustrations until 1967. While other illustrators were making their fortunes painting the blue-bloods of New York, Rockwell drew all his subjects from small American towns. He avoided professional models, using instead people from his hometown, consequently, his work had the dignity and freshness of first-hand observation.

In the 1890s "local colour" emerged as a literary trend for stories. Authors wrote about specific areas of the country they knew well, and brought out details of local customs, traditions and dialect. These were not nostalgic stories of times past. Instead, they focused on the eccentricities and prejudices of various characters drawn from the backwoods and small towns of America.

The hills of Kentucky inspired the authors James Lane Allen and John Fox, Jr. One of Lane's popular sellers was *A Kentucky Cardinal* (1895), illustrated by Albert Sterner. Fox's *Trail of the Lonesome Pine* (1908), was illustrated by Yohn who travelled to Kentucky to better understand the places and people he was to illustrate. Mary Noailles Murfree wrote about the Tennessee mountains in *The Young Mountaineers* (1897), illustrated by Malcolm Fraser. New England was the setting for Margaret Deland's *Old Chester Tales* (1899), illustrated by Howard Pyle and *Dr. Lavendar's People* (1903), illustrated by Lucius Hitchcock. Booth Tarkington's *Gentleman from Indiana* (1910), illustrated by Henry Hutt, and *The Conquest of Canaan* (1905), illustrated by Hitchcock were based on Midwestern settings. Hamlin Garland brought realism to his "local colour" stories of the Midwest. His autobiography, *Son of the Middle Border* (1914), was illustrated by Alice Barber Stephens. William Dean Howells wrote of the Ohio Valley in his book *The Leatherwood God* (1916), with a frontispiece and eight excellent illustrations by Henry Patrick Raleigh. The Far West provided the background for Bret Harte and Mary Austin. Sol Etyinge illustrated many of Harte's stories of California. Denman Fink illustrated Austin's western story *Lost Borders* (1909).

Authors of "local colour" stories, wrote in a frank, candid style about people and places in America. Likewise, the illustrators of these regional tales portrayed their characters with integrity and sincerity. For *St. Nicholas*, Gerald Leake pictured Merry from the story "Merry's Case" by Charlotte Sedgwick as a wholesome, pleasant country girl (cat. no. 92). He enhanced that image by back-lighting the character so that she seems literally a glowing picture of robust health. In another example, James Preston drew the illustration for a poem about chopping down a Christmas tree. He chose as his subjects two old-timers, red-cheeked from the cold, and dressed in layers of well-worn clothes. His spontaneous, forthright style of drawing befits the unaffected subjects at their simple task (cat. no. 115).

Whether it was images of country folk or rural landscapes, the iconography of "town and country" subjects was focused on creating a longing for something far away or long ago. These nostalgic images certainly eased the transition to a new-fangled, modern age. But after World War One there was no question but that a modern, machine age had taken hold. Country imagery seemed old-fashioned and sentimental beside the sleek and sophisticated styles of the 1920s and 1930s.

LET ME CALL YOU SWEETHEART

 ur Heroines, compared with the English, are wilding off-shoots, of a sylvan sweetness and grace and a fresh loveliness, at their best, and at their second-best such as actual women are, much too good for men, no doubt, but not such as are easily gathered in this sort of florist's window. They are scattered widely in a thousand short stories ...

William Dean Howells, *Heroines of Fiction*

[Couple fishing]
Paul C. Stahr • Cat. no. 134

ave magazines and newspapers blunted our appreciation of literary values?" was the opening question to an article in *Current Opinion* in 1915. The question was geared towards the countless lighthearted romance and adventure stories published in popular American magazines and read avidly. The article summarized the opinions of Richard Green Moulton, a literary critic of the era. "The present generation of readers ... show by their practice that they look to the newspapers and magazines as a foremost source of literary entertainment ... They can support their view by pointing to the long list of writers of first order who are contributors to journalism, and the considerable number of literary masterpieces which have appeared in periodical form."

Moulton's concern was that readers of periodicals were developing a mental habit of "sweeping swiftly over vast areas of print ... [This] mental habit once formed is turned upon other kinds of literature." He also feared the "commerical activity" of journalism would influence writers. Here he had reason for concern. Periodical literature had succeeded in luring the public into reading more. But, asked Moulton, "have they given motives for reading or impulse toward literature?"[1]

Moulton's concerns were echoed by many critics who felt that authors in America were writing stories based on their saleability — and one very lucrative area was the "romance novel." Many began as serials in one of the popular magazines with book rights being sold once the story had achieved popularity. The somewhat ornate books, with their bright cloth covers and gilded decorative borders, usually included at least a frontispiece and four to six interior illustrations — usually the same ones which were used in the magazine article. Rose O'Neill was asked to illustrate one of these sentimental romance stories which she humorously referred to as "illiterature." She told the art editor that she would only do so if she did not have to read the story. The art editor agreed, read the story for her and selected the scenes for which he wanted pictures.

Advertising the books was of great importance. Magazines not only ran book ads but pages of advertisements were also added to the backs of top-selling novels. A sampling of these ads reveals the tone and sentiment of romance literature. From Grosset & Dunlap's there was *Gret: The Story of a Pagan* (1907) by Beatrice Mantle and illustrated by Charles M. Relyea. The ad reads: "The wild free life of an Oregon lumber camp furnishes the setting for this strong original story. Gret is the daughter of the camp and is utterly content with the wild life — until love comes. A fine book, unmarred by convention." Also from Grosset & Dunlap came *The Leaven of Love* (1908) by Clara L. Burnham, illustrated by Harrison Fisher. The advertisement said: "At a Southern California resort a world-weary woman, young and beautiful but disillusioned, meets a girl who has learned the art of living — of tasting life in all its richness, opulence and joy. The story hinges upon the change wrought in the soul of the blasé woman by this glimpse into a cheery life." And from Bobbs-Merrill came *The Puppet Crown* by Harold McGrath, with illustrations by R. Maartine Reay, whose cast of characters included: "A princess rarely beautiful; a duchess magnificent and heartless; a villain revengeful and courageous; a hero youthful, humorous, fearless and truly American; such are the principal characters of this delightful story."

The stories were predictable. They had clean-cut, wholesome characters, a humorous element, and almost always a happy ending. The heroines were pretty and nearly always strong, independent women. In fact, the image Gibson had created in the "Gibson Girl" was so popular that she became the centre of many romantic tales. The men, too, were strong characters, often coming to the rescue of the "liberated damsel" when she was most in need of a hero.

The stories were set in both historical and contemporary times, and the characters were placed in small towns, high society or big cities, but whatever the time and place, the theme was always love. A few examples of bestsellers were: Mrs. Gene Stratton Porter's *Girl of Limberlost* (1909), illustrated by W.T. Benda and *The Harvester* (1911), illustrated by W.L. Jacobs; George Barr McCutcheon's *Graustark* (1901), and *Beverly of Graustark* (1904), illustrated by Harrison Fisher; Paul Leister Ford's *Tattle-Tales of Cupid* (1896), illustrated by Henry Hutt; Emerson Hough's *The Mississippi Bubble* (1902), also illustrated by Hutt; Frederic S. Isham's *Under the Rose* (1903), illustrated by Howard Chandler Christy; Kate Douglas Wiggin's *The Old Peabody Pew* (1907), illustrated by Alice Barber Stephens; Mary Hartwell Catherwood's *Lazarre* (1901), illustrated by André Castaigne, and Maurice Thompson's *Alice of Old Vincennes* (1900), illustrated by Frederick Yohn.

The authors of these amorous accounts had little influence over the illustrations. Once the story was submitted to the book or periodical publisher, it was in the hands of the art editor to chose who was best-suited to illustrate a story. Illustrators complained that inevitably when an author sent along a suggestion it was to make the heroine a "pretty girl." Even if the story did not call for a pretty girl, publishers knew that this was what the public wanted.

[Couple by the train]
Karl Anderson • Cat. no. 2

It was Charles Dana Gibson who started the phenomenon of the popular heroine with his Gibson Girl. She was tall and stately, and wore a shirtwaist style costume with her hair swept up into a loose topknot (a hairstyle also called the Gibson). She was a strong character, sociable, and self-willed. The Gibson Girl was not above fortune-hunting in her quest for a suitable marriage. In the well-known cartoon, "The Weaker Sex," the Gibson Girl is depicted with a magnifying glass and hat pin in hand, probing a tiny man, on his knees. Her female friends surround her, coolly watching her examination. When the Gibson Girl appeared in the pages of *Life* in the 1890s, it was a time of changing status for women in American society. The Gibson Girl reflected the ambiguity and dilemmas of those changes. She had a vitality and strength of character which was missing from her Victorian sisters. She freely bicycled, swam, travelled, golfed, and partied without the obligatory delicate shyness that had so long been associated with women. At the same time, the Gibson Girl also focused her goals on finding a wealthy husband and raising her social standing. Acquiring the tastes and refinements of European upper classes was considered a mark of status among the American *nouveau riche*. In Gibson's book *The Education of Mr. Pipp* (1899), the Gibson Girl demonstrated her abilities to mingle with European aristocrats. Her acceptance into titled European circles symbolized the pride of many Americans at "having arrived."

The vogue of the Gibson Girl lingered into the twentieth century. Gibson, who had worked in pen and ink, had no mastery of the tonal media of oils or watercolours. He was soon overshadowed by a new generation of illustrators who used these more versatile, popular media which could be reproduced in halftone and colour. This new generation had its own formulas for creating the American beauty. Harrison Fisher was the most popular of the illustrators of the "beau ideal." He worked principally in watercolour, turning out hundreds of drawings of graceful, elegant American women. For twenty-five years he painted covers of the "Fisher Girl" for *Cosmopolitan*. At the height of his career it was reported that Fisher made seventy-five thousand dollars a year from his illustrations alone. He sold only reproduction rights to his drawings which meant that every picture could also be used for calendars, portfolios, post cards, and gift books before he sold the original drawing to a collector. When Fisher drew the heroine for *Beverly of Graustark* (1904), a bestseller by George Barr McCutcheon, the demand for the illustration was so great that two years later the public was still asking to be sent extra copies of it.

Advertisers saw the potential for selling products using these images. The "pretty girl" pictures were not used to advertise their products directly, rather halftone prints of the famous girls were offered as incentives for consumers to purchase a product. By sending in a proof of purchase, an individual would receive a free "pretty girl" poster by one of the famous illustrators. It was enormously successful as a promotional gimmick.

The list of illustrators who had a certain type of girl associated with their work is a long one. Harrison Fisher, Henry Hutt, Howard Chandler Christy, James Montgomery Flagg, Karl Anderson, Armand Both, Hamilton King, C. Coles Phillips, Clarence F. Underwood, and Alonzo Kimball created some of the most popular types. All these artists worked from professional models. Fisher complained that he was constantly beseiged with letters from women who asked to pose for him. When the "silver screen" gained the public's attention, many artists chose models from the vast number of budding movie starlets.

Every leading lady had a leading man, and the image of the American hero was equally important to the publisher. The men pictured beside the Gibson Girls were as distinctive as the girls themselves. Tall and stately, the "Gibson Man" had broad shoulders, a firm square jaw, and an impeccable taste in clothes. Lest the male should compete with the beautiful woman, many authors turned to a different sort of man as a hero. In *Trilby* (1894), a very successful novel by George Du Maurier, the hero was described as "physically a giant, not vigorous or brilliant; he had large physical proportions and a gentle manner." It seems that good looks were not as important as communicating the nature of the man. But as the critic Laurence Burnham in an article entitled "The Modern Hero in Illustration" pointed out: "Even where the attribute of conventional good looks is absent ... there will certainly be found the compensating quality of brawn."[2]

Where the heroine was always beautiful, the hero was good-natured and able-bodied. A reviewer for *The Academy* commented that in Richard Harding Davis' book *The King's Jackle* (1891), illustrated by Gibson, "Davis is in love with strength and cleanness, with 'grit' and resource, with heroism and courage in men." Such was the ideal hero. When Arthur Keller was faced with creating the hero for Charles Steele's short story "The Right Way," he found himself with a male character not particularly handsome but "with a large heart and soul, tremendous force, and versatility of mind." Keller confessed that after much thought he had modelled the hero after a prominent New York man who was much in the public eye. Although this man did not actually pose for the pictures, the public identity which readers associated with him was transferred to the hero of the story.

The most popular of all "hero creators" was Joseph Leyendecker. He was commissioned to do an advertisement for shirts with detachable collars called Arrow Shirts. He chose as his model Charles Beach, a Canadian who became his lifetime companion. The Arrow Shirt man was handsome, well-built, and had an Ivy League wardrobe. Leyendecker used a technique in which a grid was drawn on the canvas, and a smaller grid was drawn on the preparatory sketch. There by transferring the sketch square by square to the canvas grid, a precise copy of the original sketch was achieved. The results were a clean, geometric image of a starched, but virile man. This portrait was enormously successful for the Arrow Shirt Company. Female fans (who, after all, probably bought most of the shirts for the men in their lives) wrote letters by the thousands and sent gifts and marriage proposals to their ideal man. Leyendecker had a long, successful career in all areas of illustration, but even now is most clearly associated with the Arrow Shirt Man.

References to sexual associations between men and women in either the text or pictures were strictly taboo. In fact, female magazine readers were insulted by advertisements for corsets and long underwear in magazines. When the *Woman's Home Companion* used the term "woman" instead of "lady," readers com-plained that "woman" was a vulgar term. The *Ladies' Home Journal* announced a contest to pick the ideal female reader of the *Journal*. The winner would pose for Charles Dana Gibson. The rules discreetly announced that all photographs submitted must have both the consent of the girl and her parents before it would be considered. Letters of complaint poured in from offended parents. In the next issue the contest was abruptly halted with an elaborate apology from the editor. It seems that female readers desired to look at the popular-type girls but not be identified as one.

In the decade following World War One, the images changed radically. John Held parodied the change in a cartoon called "Thirty Years of Progress" where a girl in a short skirt, rolled stockings, flask in hand, flicks a cigarette ash at a prim and proper Gibson Girl, who had seemed so shocking with her independent ways a generation before. Now, she was no match for the flapper.

NOTES

1. "Have Magazines and Newspapers Blunted Our Appreciation of Literary Values?" *Current Opinion*, vol. 59 (1915), p. 427.
2. Laurence Burnham, "The Modern Hero in Illustration," *The Bookman*, vol. 25 (1907), p. 506.

DEEDS OF DERRING DO

oaring, screaming, clanking, the runaways thundered down upon them. Alex sprang back from the whirling handles and faced about. The foreman edged by them and joined them. Nearer, towering above them, rushed the leading car. "Now be sure and jump high and grab hard," shouted the foreman. "Ready! JUMP!"

F. Lovell Coombs, "The Runaway Train"

" 'There is none aboard the Sunda shall command her now!'..."
Percy Elton Cowan • Cat. no. 37

eddy Roosevelt was an advocate of a life filled with toil and risk. He feared that the prosperity Americans were experiencing in the late nineteenth century would lead to a nation of soft, lax people. Roosevelt rode with the "Rough Riders" in Cuba, hunted game in Africa, toured the Panama Canal under construction, harpooned devilfish in Florida, took strenuous hikes near his home on Long Island, and rafted on the Amazon River in Brazil, to mention only a few of his adventures. When asked why he took the Brazilian trip he said, "It was my last chance to be a boy."

Perhaps it was a desire to recapture youth that made stories of adventure so popular in the decades surrounding the turn of the century. For those whose lives were devoid of great adventures, the next best thing was reading about heros and heroines of great courage.

"The door swung back, and a knight stood there."
Maurice L. Bower • Cat. no. 18

These stories also complemented the amorous and fanciful tales which were in abundance at the time. Publishers geared these adventure stories toward a male audience, although female readers devoured them with nearly the same vigour as men.

This vigourous school of writers chose lively and provocative settings for their stories such as Africa, South America, the Orient, or the Yukon Territory. Within the United States, the states and territories of the West still held the allure of a wild region inhabited by steely, rugged individuals. By 1890, the West was, in fact, considerably tamer than authors described it, yet the public demanded these "wild and woolly" adventures with vivid, dramatic pictures to fire their imagination. Bill Cody, for example, saw his image as rendered by an illustrator, and only then did he don the familiar leather-fringed costume associated with a cowboy.[1] Artist Frank Schoonover was asked by the popular author Clarence E. Mulford to find a cowboy who had a stumped leg, and to send him sketches to help create a character Mulford had in mind. Schoonover found such a man and thus was born the legendary Hopalong Cassidy.[2] The character Molly from Emerson Hough's "The Covered Wagon" was rendered by illustrator W.H.D. Koerner. So memorable was Molly's image as the pioneer woman that when the film version was cast, an actress who matched the illustration was chosen.[3]

Authors and illustrators together created an American folklore centred on cowboys, Indians, pioneers, and a whole romanticized cast of characters. Illustrators of the West such as Frank Schoonover, N.C. Wyeth, W.H.D. Koerner, and Harvey Dunn actually visited the West and lived the lives of cowboys. Their drawings and paintings have the veracity of their creators having been there. They were illustrators of fiction and fittingly added aggrandisement and sentimentality to their characters and settings.

A few publishers tried to illustrate western novels with photographs alone, but the public demand for more colourful imagery assured the illustrators of continuing assignments. Frederic Remington, Charles Russell and Maynard Dixon were often assigned "picture stories" that appeared as double-page spreads in magazines and told a story without a text. These artists aimed to document scenes from frontier life. They took photographs and purchased props to help them remember the details when they returned to their studios. Yet for all the illustrators' efforts to record the West as it really was, eastern publishers were usually interested in more melodramatic images of the frontier. Maynard Dixon complained that he did not like to lie about the West, and he gave up illustrating for that reason.[4]

Historical fiction on themes of courage and valour was another literary vogue of this period. Authors brought to life the spirit and daring of real and imaginary figures from the past. Popular sellers about the American Revolutionary were: Winston Churchill's *Richard Carvell* (1899), illustrated by Carlton T. Chapman and Malcolm Fraser; and Paul Leister Ford's *Janice Meredith* (1899), illustrated by Howard Pyle. Irving Bacheller's *D'ri and I* (1901), was a historical romance and adventure story of the War of 1812, illustrated by Frederick C. Yohn. Frank Stockton wrote swashbuckling stories of pirates in *Buccaneers and Pirates of Our Coast* (1898), illustrated by George Varian and B.W. Clinedinst. The adventures of pioneers in Tennessee were the subject of Mary N. Murfree's bestseller, *The Story of Old Fort Loudon* (1899), illustrated by Ernest Peixotto. Kentucky in 1863 was the setting for James Lane Allen's *The Sword of Youth* (1915). This story, like most bestsellers, had appeared serially in a popular magazine before the book was published. John Wolcott Adams furnished a frontispiece and twenty pen and ink sketches which enliven the adventures of country life.

Writers and illustrators of children's books and periodicals also contributed good adventure stories. *St. Nicholas Magazine* attracted such noted adventure authors as: Teddy Roosevelt, Bret Harte, Jack London, F. Lovell Coombs, and Richard Harding Davis. *Scribner's* published tales of medieval lore by author-illustrator, Howard Pyle. The success of Pyle's *Otto of the Silver Hand* (1888), and the *Merry Adventures of Robin Hood* (1883), led to the well-known series of books on the legends of King Arthur: *Story of King Arthur and His Knights* (1903), *Story of the Champions of the Round Table* (1905), *Story of Sir Lancelot and His Companions* (1907), and *Story of the Grail and the Passing of Arthur* (1910). Pyle incorporated the style of Albrecht Dürer with his own to achieve an old masters' look to these drawings. Maurice Bower was also attracted to the medieval period. His debt to his teacher, Howard Pyle, is evident in his painstaking accuracy to detail. His illustrations for the magazine story, "The Adventure of the High King" (1919), by Clara Platt Meadowcraft, also captured the mood of a bygone era (cat. no. 18).

Several Pyle students specialized in the illustration of adventure. N.C. Wyeth was commissioned by *Scribner's* to do the illustrations for a series called *Scribner's Illustrated Classics*. Wyeth's best work was done for these books. There were frequent new editions with his illustrations. Children today who are just discovering such classics as: Robert Louis Stevenson's *Treasure Island* (1911) and *Kidnapped* (1913), Jules Verne's

"Dutch sat down and fanned himself with his hat..."
Charles Nicolas Sarka • Cat. no. 126
(reproduced in colour p. 52)

Mysterious Island (1918), and James Fenimore Cooper's *Last of the Mohicans* (1919), can enjoy reprints of N.C. Wyeth's illustrations. Harper and Brothers recognized the success of the Scribner's classics' series and in 1921 started its own series. Another Pyle student, Frank Schoonover, was asked to do the illustrations for fourteen cover designs. Among the works he illustrated were: *Gulliver's Travels, Kidnapped, Robinson Crusoe,* and *Swiss Family Robinson.*

It is not surprising that many of Howard Pyle's students excelled in picturing deeds of derring-do. Pyle told his students to capture the most dramatic moment and emphasize that drama through composition and colour. A tightly-framed scene with strong diagonal lines and a tipped-up picture plane characterized Pyle's students' works. Like Pyle's own style of shimmering colour effects, his students used colour to endow a composition with energy. Noteworthy among his pupils who mastered adventure illustration were: Harvey Dunn, Stanley Arthurs, Walter Hunt Everett, Clyde Osmer De Land, Philip R. Goodwin, George Harding, and Harry Townsend.

Outside of the Pyle circle — but equally dramatic illustrators of adventure were: Charles Sarka, George Gibbs, and Percy Cowen. Sarka travelled a great deal and was assigned stories which were set in exotic places. For the story "Tenderfoot goes Alligator Hunting" (1910) in *Success Magazine,* Charles Sarka convincingly created a scene of sweltering heat in an alligator infested swamp (cat. no. 126). Sarka preferred to work in watercolour and in his hands this delicate medium took on vibrancy and power. His drawings flicker with strong light effects created by blank spaces of white paper next to the strokes and washes of watercolour.

George Gibbs wrote and illustrated many of his own stories which gave him the advantage of creating characters and scenes exactly as he had written them. "The Revenge of Decatur" (1901) from *Cosmopolitan Magazine,* is a story set during the War of 1812 (cat. no. 65). For his illustration, Gibbs picked the dramatic moment of boarding the enemy ship. He arranged the composition so that the reader's perspective is directly behind the main figure. It is as if the reader is plunged into the conflict himself.

Percy Cowen also used composition to create a sense of adventure. A close-up scene of two men in a heated argument from "The Blood of Admirals" (1915) in *Collier's Magazine,* is a good example (cat. no. 37). Cowen captured the tension of a mutiny. The viewer focuses on the overpowering face of a man, both hands clenched in iron-like fists, leaning towards an officer who retreats in astonishment. It is the kind of scene that a good illustrator such as Cowen did well. The picture is so engrossing that one wonders what has happened just before, and what will happen next. That, after all, was the function of all illustrations — to grab the reader's attention but not give away the plot.

NOTES

1. Teona Tone Gneiting, "Literature and Art for the Masses: The Dime Novel," *The American Personality,* University of California, Los Angeles, (1976), p. 25.
2. Ann Barton Brown, *Frank E. Schoonover Illustrator,* Brandywine River Museum, (1979), p. 26.
3. W.H. Hutchinson, *W.H.D. Koerner, Illustrator of the West,* Los Angeles County Museum of Natural History, (1968), p. 6.
4. Joseph E. Young, "The American Frontier," *The American Personality,* University of California, Los Angeles, (1976), p. 61.

MYSTERY AND SUSPENSE

his is something more than a mere detective story; it is a thrilling romance — a romance mystery and crime where a shrewd detective helps solve the mystery. The characters most liked but longest suspected are proved not only guiltless, but above suspicion. It is a story to be read with a rush and at a sitting, for no one can put it down until the mystery is solved.

Advertisement for *The Filigree Ball*, by Anna Katherine Green

"While the Grandfather clock ticked ten times..."
Alice Barber Stephens • Cat. no. 135

he suspense story had the appeal of the adventure tale, but with an added twist of murder, mystery, and an intricate plot. The popularity of detective stories was the outgrowth of crowded city-living in which America for the first time faced rising crime rates. Even the country dwellers were beginning to lock their doors at night. In the 1890s, author Julian Hawthorne commented with astonishment and dismay about the new vogue of ladies attending murder trials. The first "Nick Carter" detective dime novel appeared in 1890, followed by an incredible one thousand and seventy-six stories centred around this character. Crime literature was evolving in the 1890s, but it was the authors of the twentieth century who brought this genre to life.

Many of these detective yarns and murder mysteries were issued serially, and editors were committed to keeping the climax and conclusion a secret. Illustrators were given only the pertinent parts of a manuscript so that they would not expose the outcome and spoil the story. The editors of these mysteries depended on the illustrators to lure the reader into the story. A gun pointed at a fair heroine, the villain choking the hero, the brawling fistfight — all these action-filled pictures piqued the reader's curiosity, hopefully enough to read the story. Violence did not carry the taboo of sex. Although grim and gory details were avoided, there was a good measure of violence in American illustration at the turn of the century.

Illustrators had their own methods of creating the action in a dramatic scene. Arthur William Brown was a typical example. First, he read the manuscript quickly for the story line and then again more carefully, making notes of potential scenes and character descriptions. He hired models to suit the story line, collected the necessary costumes and props in his studio, and then set the scene much like a stage director would a play. Once he felt the models had captured the action and proper emotions, he photographed them. Close-up shots, as well as various angles, were helpful in the final drawing. Special supports were used for action scenes that required characters to run, jump or fall. Three bricks under the front foot and a fan blowing the hair back from the face looked close enough to a run to be convincing. Once all the photographs were developed, Brown chose the ones he would use. Often the final illustration was completed with the character of one, the action of another, and the facial expressions of a third.

Norman Rockwell used from seventy-five to one hundred photographs for each painting he composed. Many artists resisted using photographs because it was believed that a good illustrator did not need to resort to mechanical aids. But periodical illustrators usually had only four weeks or less to complete a finished drawing. Thus, many turned to photography as well as other time saving techniques.

The pantograph was a device commonly used by newspapermen, that reduced or enlarged a photograph to a traceable size. Brown used the pantograph to enlarge his sketches onto a bigger sheet of paper in order to block in the composition. Other illustrators used an opaque projector and sketched directly onto a primed canvas. Maxfield Parrish developed his own special equipment, much like a slide projector, to create paintings with perfectly symmetrical, balanced compositions.

George Wright was a master of the suspense-filled picture. He had an innate sense for picking the most dramatic moment and then highlighting the action through light effects and composition. For example, the choking scene from the short story "Banjo Nell" by James Hooper, is lighted from the base of the scene, throwing a looming shadow on the wall (cat. no. 150). The shadow takes on the form of a grostesque monster, a fitting echo of the villain's character. From the short story "The Harvest Moon" by Justus Miles Foreman, Wright did an illustration of a woman rising from her chair, her hand over her face, as her gentleman companion sits coolly, obviously embarrassed by her outburst (cat. no. 151). In fact, the illustration alludes to a very minor point in the story, but the curious drama of the picture alone pulls the reader in.

Various illustrators achieved dramatic effects in unique ways. M. Leone Bracker, for example, provided the frontispiece to Francis Marion Crawford's suspense story *Wandering Ghosts*, (1911). He used eerie lighting effects to achieve his drama. A single lighting source chisels out the deeply furrowed faces of two astonished men staring into an empty hat box (cat. no. 20). Edmund Ashe manipulated the composition to evoke a startled feeling in his audience. The viewer finds himself looking down the barrels of two barkers in an illustration for "The Man in Black" by H.B. Marriott Watson (cat. no. 3). Fanny Young Cory creates an alarming situation using both lighting and composition. An old lady peers down the hallway, candle in hand. A shadow twice her size ominiously hovers behind her (cat. no. 36). In each case the illustrator successfully accomplished his purpose — to make the casual magazine scanner stop and read the story.

Many authors capitalized on Americans' fascination with crime. One of the first detective characters to become popular in America was "Raffles," the creation of British author E.W. Hornung. Frederick Yohn did the

"What?...It's gone, man, the skull is gone!!"
M. Leone Bracker • Cat. no. 20

illustrations for: *Raffles; Further Adventures* (1901). Anna Katherine Green was the author of *The Filigree Ball* (1903), illustrated by Charles Reylea. She followed this success with *Mayor's Wife* (1907), illustrated by Alice Barber Stephens; *The Leavenworth Case* (1913), illustrated by Gerald W. Peters; *Golden Slipper* (1915), illustrated by Arthur Keller; and several other titles. Jacques Futrelle wrote: *The Chase of the Golden Plate* (1906), illustrated by Will Grefe; *The Diamond Master* (1909), illustrated by Herman Pfeifer; and *My Lady's Garter* (1912), illustrated by Frederico Gruger. Mary Roberts Rinehart added romance to her mysteries in: *The Circular Staircase* (1908), illustrated by Lester Ralph; *The Man in Lower Ten* (1909), illustrated by

Howard Chandler Christy; and *The Case of Jennie Brice* (1913), illustrated by M. Leone Bracker. Carolyn Wells created the detective character Fleming Stone for her mysteries. *The Clue*, illustrated by Francis Rogers, was published in 1909. Melville Davisson Post wrote *The Strange Schemes of Randolph Mason* in 1896. Post also wrote the *Gilded Chair* (1910), illustrated by Albert Wenzell and Arthur Becher. Paul Stahr illustrated two mysteries for Isabel Ostrander — *The Clue in the Air* (1917), and *Anything Once* (1920).

These primers in detective stories and murder mysteries formed the basis for a thriving literary genre which continues to captivate readers today.

THE GREAT OUTDOORS

 [Buck] walked to the center of the open space and listened. It was the call, the many-noted call, sounding more luring and compelling than ever before. And as never before, he was ready to obey. John Thornton was dead. The last tie was broken. Man and the claims of man no longer bound him.

Jack London, *The Call of the Wild*

"Building the lynx cabane"
Frank Earle Schoonover • Cat. no. 129
(reproduced in colour p. 56)

he adventure of exploring the wilderness, the majesty of seeing wild animals, and the romance of escaping to the unspoiled, open spaces of America were appealing to both young and old readers. President Theodore Roosevelt initiated a program of land conservation and reclamation. He protected one hundred and forty-eight acres of national forests, set aside five national parks and declared nearly one and a half million acres as national monuments, and established wildlife refuges. He was also an advocate of enjoying the great outdoors and encouraged other Americans to do the same.

Stories about the great outdoors were popular features of both magazines and books. The periodical *Outing* was devoted to outdoor life. It featured not only advice on camping, hiking, fishing, hunting, and other outdoor sports, but also descriptions of the vast natural wonders found in America. Other magazines such as *American Boy* and *St. Nicholas Magazine* ran regular stories on natural history.

The period also produced writers such as Charles G.D. Roberts, Jack London, Ernest Thompson Seton, John Burroughs, Samuel Scoville, Harold McCracken, and Dallas Lore Sharp, all of whom wrote about wildlife. These authors looked for illustrators who could draw animals with accuracy and capture the furor and excitement of a wildlife story.

One illustrator who stood out among the rest was Charles Livingston Bull. Having developed a love for animals as a child, Bull began his career as a taxidermist. He studied taxidermy at the Ward's Museum in Rochester, New York, and took drawing classes in the evenings at the Mechanic's Institute. At the Institute Bull met architect Harvey Ellis. Ellis was a follower of the Arts and Crafts Movement, and a collector of both Japanese woodcuts and English Art Nouveau prints. Bull was influenced greatly by Ellis' tastes and style of drawing. Although Bull's artwork is stylized and decorative, there is a painstaking honesty to it which reflects his respect for animal life.

Bull's drawings were in great demand. Publishers would hold books from press, waiting for Bull to find time to provide the illustrations. He worked first from sketches, establishing the format of the drawings in his studio. Afternoons were spent at the zoo observing animals. There he waited patiently to catch the animals in action so that he could correct his sketches and add the detail. He was friendly with the zookeepers who sometimes co-operated in stimulating the animals to move for Bull. On one occasion, for example, Bull needed to render a flock of peafowl in flight. The Keeper of Birds at the Bronx Zoo arranged for all the peafowl to be dropped from a tall building on the zoo grounds.[1] After his sketches were as accurate as possible, Bull finished the work in his studio.

Bull acquired so great a knowledge from his observations at the zoo, and from expeditions he undertook to Mexico and South America, he sometimes submitted corrections for the text of the books he was illustrating. When Jack London published his well-known book *The Call of the Wild* (1903), Bull was teamed with illustrator Philip R. Goodwin to provide the drawings. The second edition in 1912 was illustrated by Paul Bransom. Although Bransom specialized in animal illustrations, he declared Bull was an artist, whereas he was merely an illustrator.

Paul Bransom, ten years Bull's junior, began his illustration career as a comic strip artist. Like Bull, he loved animals and spent his spare time sketching at the zoo in New York. The artist Walter Kuhn encouraged Bransom to devote his artistic skills to animal illustration. The *Saturday Evening Post* bought four cover designs of animals subjects from him. These early animal illustrations led to Bransom receiving his first animal story to illustrate. The New York Zoological Park arranged for him to have a studio on the zoo grounds, a privilege that greatly facilitated his work.

Two other noteworthy natural history artists are Walter King Stone and Robert Bruce Horsfall. Stone borrowed heavily from Bull's style, working in flat, decorative designs. Many of Stone's drawings show animals not as the primary subjects, but as part of the landscape. His drawings often appeared in *Scribner's, Century*, and *Harper's*. Horsfall, on the other hand, rendered animals in a straightforward, realistic style. His drawings accompanied the many scientific articles in *St. Nicholas Magazine*, which were intended as educational reading for children (cat. no. 81). Horsfall was the last of a long line of American natural history illustrators who recorded with scientific accuracy the animal life in America. With the coming of photography, magazines relied heavily on the camera lens for their pictures, and artists like Horsfall found themselves with fewer and fewer assignments.

NOTES

1. Peter White, *Charles Livingston Bull*, Glenbow Museum, (Calgary, 1979), p. 11.

"Ef we don't make Conroy's camp purty soon..."
Paul Bransom • Cat. no. 23

DREAM DAYS

y ambition in days gone by was to write a really notable adult book, but now I am glad that I have made literary friends of the children rather than older folk. In one's mature years, one forgets the books that one reads, but the stories of childhood leave an indelible impression, and their author always has a niche in the temple of memory, from which the image is never cast out to be thrown into the rubbish-heap of things that are outlived.

Howard Pyle from a letter to Merle Johnson

"The Adventure of the Knight of the Singing Sword"
Maurice L. Bower • Cat no. 19

hildren's books and periodicals are the publications in which one would expect to find lavish illustrations. The pictures in children's books are more than mere ornamentation — they help the children understand the text and entice them to read more.

Publishers in colonial and early Federal America published many illustrated children's books pirated from English editions. Copperplate engravers and wood engravers copied the plates and cuts, occasionally adding details to make the books seem more American. By the 1830s, children's book publications were dominated by the American Sunday School Union and the American Tract Society. Although moral teaching was of primary importance, both organizations were dedicated to improving children's literature by encouraging stories about American children. Rollo, created by Jacob Abbott, was the first native boy to appear in American juvenile literature. But the stories about Rollo were dull and moralizing. In breaking away from foreign traditions in young people's stories, authors and illustrators of American juvenile literature lost much of the folklore and spiritual mystery present in European literature. Gone were the fairy tales and nonsense verses. American children's books in the nineteenth century were pedantic and moralizing, nearly always containing a religious message for the young reader.

It was the exceptional author who broke with this format and wrote stories about realistic children. Three examples were: Mary Mapes Dodge's *Hans Brinker, or The Silver Skates* (1865), Thomas Bailey Aldrich's *Story of a Bad Boy* (1869), and Louisa May Alcott's *Little Women* (1868). However, illustrators were slow in adapting to the authors' new realism. Alcott complained about Hammett Billings' drawings for her story, claiming that he had not captured the spontaneity of her characters. It was the authors' demands on illustrators that helped upgrade illustrations in American children's books.

The same craze for periodical literature that captivated adult audience in the late 1870s, also enchanted the juvenile audience. *Our Young Folks* was started in 1865 and continued for eleven years. *The Riverside Magazine for Young People* ran from 1867 to 1871. Harper's contributed *Harper's Young People* from 1879 to 1899. *Youth's Companion* was a weekly magazine published in Boston and for many years was that city's only magazine to achieve a large national circulation.

The most popular and successful of all juvenile periodicals was *St. Nicholas Magazine*, which issued its first number in 1873 under the superb editorship of Mary Mapes Dodge. Her aim from the beginning was to bring quality to the pages of children's literature. She believed children did not want to be talked down to or preached at. Instead, they wanted a magazine which they could call their own. Evidence that she succeeded in pleasing her young readers is found in *St. Nicholas Magazine* large subscription list and in the many positive letters to the editor published in each issue.

St. Nicholas Magazine was published by the Century Company, providing Dodge a network of writers and illustrators from which to choose. Some were reluctant at first, holding fast to the out-dated opinion that children's writers and illustrators were inferior. But during Dodge's tenure she lured to the magazine such important authors as: Rudyard Kipling, Frank Stockton, Tudor Jenks, Carolyn Wells, Frances Hodgson Burnett, Jack London, Cornelia Meigs, Rachel Field, John Kendrick Bangs, and Laura Richards. Illustrators included such greats as Reginald Birch, Howard Pyle, Gelett Burgess, Norman Price, George Wharton Edwards, Alice Barber Stephens, Oliver Herford, and Charles Relyea.

Many of the successful stories for *St. Nicholas Magazine* became the classics of American children's literature; some still attract children today. Frances Hodgson Burnett's *Little Lord Fauntleroy* was serialized first in *St. Nicholas Magazine*. The book was published in 1886. Reginald Birch was selected as illustrator because his delicate pen and ink style suited the flavour of the book. He provided twelve ink wash and watercolour drawings, and twenty-four pen and ink vignettes. He was paid sixty dollars for the full-page illustrations, and twenty-four dollars for the smaller inset illustrations; an amount totalling twelve hundred dollars.[1] Burnett provided the illustrator with a photograph of her son, dressed in the velvet breeches, lace ruffles and long curls which were popular in the 1880s. The popularity of the book reinforced the "Lord Fauntleroy" style of dress, and many a young American boy found himself posed before a camera in the familiar costume.

Another tremendous success in *St. Nicholas Magazine* was the "Brownies" (cat. nos. 38-43). Created by the illustrator Palmer Cox, these creatures were based on Scottish folkloric characters who, in contrast to the fairies, were the swarthy folk who came out after the family had gone to sleep and did the chores that had been left undone during the day. The Brownies were high-spirited folk, and mixed with their good deeds was a lot of rascally fun. Cox drew the Brownies as bulbous creatures with large eyes, thin arms and legs. Each character had a different name — the Arab, the Chinaman, the Policeman, the Dude, even a Teddy Roosevelt Brownie. The Brownies went everywhere as a

[Brownies under a Haystack]
Palmer Cox • Cat. no. 40

group, and the verses that accompanied the pictures promoted patriotism, diligence, and loyalty. Cox filled the
pages of eleven books with these characters, as well as
promoting a line of toys, games, spoons, candy moulds,
and other gimmickry. It is difficult to imagine that it
was didactic verse which drew children to these
creatures. Rather, one would expect that these tricksters
as humorous images were a refreshing change from the
heavy-handed fare of other children's books. Their
popularity lasted more than twenty-five years.

Howard Pyle was a noteworthy name in children's literature at the end of the nineteenth century. He went to New York in 1876 at the age of twenty-three, determined to pursue a career as an illustrator. His talent was recognized by Charles Parsons, the art editor at *Harper's*. Pyle became part of the distinguished team of illustrators which included: Edwin Abbey, Arthur Burdett Frost, William T. Smedley, and Charles Reinhart. After establishing himself as a top illustrator, Pyle moved back to his native city, Wilmington, Delaware. Pyle divided his time between illustrating and teaching at Drexel Institute in Philadelphia. Frustrated by the teaching policies at Drexel, he decided to begin his own experimental art school in Chadds Ford, Pennsylvania. Students who applied for admission to this school were interviewed by Pyle, who carefully reviewed samples of their artwork. After he had chosen about a

dozen of the top applicants, this select few took up residence in a converted old mill on the Brandywine River. They lived together, picnicked in the countryside, and took bicycle trips — all under the careful tutelage of Pyle.

Pyle's teaching was not centred on the technical skills of modelling, perspective, or composition. He presumed that the students who came to him already had artistic talent and training in the fundamentals of drawing and painting. What Pyle taught his students was a point-of-view. Illustration, he believed, should be a reflection of the world the artist knew intimately. A well-known example of this philosophy in action took place during a picnic. Pyle had a student wade into a cold stream so he would truly know what it felt like to be freezing. "Project your mind into your subject," he told his students. "Let your soul flow into your pictures."

"The little lady of the Manor 'Blesses' the Grand old Apple Orchard"
Marjorie Torre and T.M. Bevans • Cat. no. 12

He urged his students to collect old costumes and props to lend the correct historical mood to their pictures. Students such as Frank Schoonover and N.C. Wyeth took his advice very seriously and travelled extensively to get a feeling for the settings of stories they were illustrating.

There was no one style that characterized the work of Pyle's students. Rather, there was a tone or an attitude which connected him to his students, demonstrated by an honesty and spirit in their work. There was also a willingness to experiment — to break away from the formulas which older illustrators had so firmly established. Many of Pyle's students composed their pictures from new viewpoints, taking advantage of the extremely foreshortened picture plane to create a feeling of drama or excitement. N.C. Wyeth often used a composition in which the action of the picture appeared to be rushing into our own space. It was a very effective device because it quickly caught children's attention.

Several of Pyle's female students chose a decorative style influenced by the Art Nouveau style, Japanese prints, and Pyle's own borrowings from Dürer and other old-master printmakers. This style was characterized by broad, flat areas enclosed with heavy black outlines. Jessie Willcox Smith's work best illustrates this decorative style in her very popular drawings of children. Charlotte Harding [Brown], Elizabeth Shippen Green [Elliott], Ellen Wetherald Ahrens, Anna Whelan Betts, Bertha Corson Day [Bates], Olive Rush, Sarah S. Stilwell [Weber], Ada Williamson, and Sarah K. Smith used similar styles. Each of these women had successful careers as illustrators.

Maxfield Parrish was a Pyle student for a short period, but he came to the master having already formulated a style which was unique and appealing. Parrish can take credit for bringing a spirit of enchantment and fantasy to American children's illustrations. The subjects of his paintings were romantic castles, sylvan landscapes, Arabian palaces, and rustic, peaceful environments. His colours were brilliant and vibrant — perfect colours for creating a dreamlike aura. His drawings combined line, stipple, and wash, often with collage to add interesting textures. Noteworthy among the children's books which he illustrated were: Kenneth Grahame's *Dream Days* (1902), and *Golden Age* (1900); Eugene Field's *Poems of Childhood* (1904), and *Arabian Nights* (1909).

One of the most beloved classics of American juvenile literature, *The Wonderful Wizard of Oz* (1900), was written and illustrated during this period. L. Frank Baum wrote the story based on the bedtime tales he had told his own children. His friend, William Wallace Denslow, did the illustrations. The story was the first popular fairy tale to take place in America. Dorothy, the heroine, travels to Oz, an enchanted land very much like the utopian dreams immigrants had about America.[2] The illustrations were simple line drawings with flat primary colours. It is the simplicity and directness of style which made these drawings so appealing to children.

Peter Newell was the illustrator who brought picture books to life. German publishers excelled in making toybooks, and McLoughlin Brothers in America copied many German designs with success. Newell was most certainly aware of McLoughlin's shape books, pop-ups and moveable pages when he designed his toybooks. The three most successful of his books were: *The Hole Book* (1908), *The Slant Book* (1910), and *The Rocket Book* (1912). *The Hole Book* was about a boy who accidentally fired a gun, the bullet travelled through the actual pages of the book, and created fun and mischief as it went. *The Rocket Book* followed the path of a rocket set off in the basement of an apartment building. The book had a hole on every page where the rocket had done its damage. *The Slant Book* was shaped as a parallelogram so that the pages of the book formed the slope for the journey of a baby in his carriage, released from Nanny's care. Newell had a unassuming, seemingly untrained style of drawing. Similar to Denslow's style, it was their unadulterated simplicity that made these books so memorable to many generations of American children.

Quality writing and illustration, and an attitude of fun and entertainment were the hallmarks of children's literature at the turn of the century. Parents, authors, illustrators, and teachers gained a better understanding of a child's needs and desires. Gone forever were the dull, lifeless, sententious books of the past. In their place were books and magazines whose aims were variety, merit, and a spirit of fun.

NOTES

1. The Scribner's files on illustrators, archives of the Brandywine River Museum in Chadds Ford, Pennsylvania.
2. Selma G. Lanes in her book *Down the Rabbit Hole* (New York, 1976) points out the parallels between Oz and American society at the turn of the century.

WAR!

You go with your army, often with the Germans behind you while whole companies have wedged through the enemy, often leaving the Boche behind, so that as you pass through villages, you find many Germans still there, sniping at you from the windows. You go on and on, until at last you realize that you have absolutely lost all power of observation and that everything appears common-place. It gradually sinks into your tired mind that you need sleep, a hot meal and a chance to get the stuff you've seen out of your head. Then you drop behind, get a good sleep, something to eat, and a large piece of paper to work on, which is a relief after the six-by-eight sketchbook. Then you get out again for the big show.

George Harding from "The American Artist at the Front"

"My guardian was looking down at me..."
Wallace Morgan • Cat. no. 99

etween 1890 and 1925 America was involved in two wars — the Spanish-American War and World War One. The people back home were eager for war news, but the photographs that were sent back were not an adequate source for understanding the human reaction to the wars. Families and friends wanted to know the mood of the war. They wanted to know where the boys slept, what they ate, and how they felt in the midst of an attack. Cameras could not capture those kinds of personal glimpses. For this the publishers relied on the artist war-correspondent.

This type of artist-report was familiar to Americans who had lived during the American Civil War. "Special Artists," as the periodicals referred to them, were sent to the front to make sketches of the action. These sketches were transported to wood engravers working in the safety of New York. An artist copied them onto a wooden plank, which was divided into small blocks and given to several wood engravers to cut the design. They were then pieced back together and attached with wooden dowels. A final engraver connected the lines to finish the whole drawing. By dividing the labour, publishers saved time, so battle pictures of the Civil War were available sometimes only a day after an event had occurred.

When William McKinley became President in 1897, America's economy was stable, and McKinley wished to keep it that way. The Cubans were fighting for their independence from Spain, and the clashes between the two were turbulent and brutal. In the frenzied years of 1895 to 1898, Americans tried diplomacy with Spain, urging it to recognize Cuban independence. These negotiations might have succeeded if the American warship, the *Maine*, had not been mysteriously blown up in the port of Havanna. That incident, combined with the blatant "yellow journalism" of the press, sparked American indignation. On April 25, 1898, Congress voted a state of war with Spain.

The war immediately created its own heroes. Admiral George Dewey in the Pacific scored a swift victory against Spanish warships, preventing them from reaching Cuba. "Fighting Joe" Wheeler volunteered for duty at the age of sixty-one. He wore the "Union Blues" to battle, a symbol of his loyalty to the United States although he had fought for the Confederacy during the Civil War. Theodore Roosevelt and his "Rough Riders" captivated the imagination of Americans who followed their exploits in newspapers. As an example of the power of the press, combined with illustrations,

Roosevelt was in Cuba only about a week, yet the publicity brought him national attention and soon, the vice-presidency.

The war also brought fame to some novice illustrators who covered the action. Most famous was Howard Chandler Christy. Christy followed the "Rough Riders," and the pictures he sent back to the United States were published by *Harper's, Scribner's,* and *Leslie's Weekly.* Christy became so well-established as a war illustrator that when he returned home, publishers continued to give him only war stories to illustrate. Eager to move on to the more glamorous illustrations of society life and beautiful girls, Christy pleaded with his publishers to give him more variety in his assignments. He eventually succeeded in getting glamorous stories, and ultimately achieved long-lasting fame as a "pretty girl" artist.

Frederic Remington was commissioned by William Randolph Hearst to draw sketches of Cuba. It was rumoured that Remington told Hearst that the conditions in Cuba did not merit violence. Hearst replied, "You furnish the pictures and I'll furnish the war." Remington accompanied author Richard Harding Davis to Cuba. Together they created written and visual records which are regarded as important documentations of the war.

Frederick Yohn wanted to illustrate the war, but ill health brought him only as close as the camps, before he was obliged to return to New York. *Collier's* had commissioned him to draw pictures for its coverage of the war, and he was determined to do so. From his studio in New York, Yohn read about the war in cable dispatches and in newspapers. He drew his illustrations from these accounts and from his vivid imagination. He recalled the time in his studio, in an interview in 1927:

> I was doing my work in a room on Twenty-fourth Street. Often there would be a cab waiting at the door to rush the finished picture away. It used to amuse me at times to see them when they appeared because they were always labelled, 'By our own correspondent, drawn on the spot.' The spot happened to be my room on Twenty-fourth Street.[1]

He drew thirty-six illustrations of the Spanish-American War for *Collier's*.

The years following the Spanish-American War were relatively peaceful. President Wilson avoided war with Mexico during the Mexican Civil War and fought with great courage to keep Americans neutral in World War One which erupted in Europe in 1914. But in April 1917, after agonizing over his decision to join the conflict or keep America at peace, Wilson asked Congress to declare war. His speech before a joint session of Congress stirred the American spirit as he declared that the world must be made "safe for democracy."

The illustrator Charles Dana Gibson took the responsibility of organizing American artists towards the war effort. He used the Society of Illustrators as his base and called upon illustrators to contribute poster designs which would promote the war cause. At first the government was reluctant to get involved with Gibson and his committee. But through Gibson's persuasive powers and the knowledge that the poster campaign was a positive force in shaping American attitudes, the government formed the Division of Pictures of the Committee on Public Information on the War Department. Major Kendall Banning was the military director for the division, and Gibson, as a civilian, headed up the committee.

[Woman nursing a wounded soldier]
Henry Hutt • Cat. no. 82

The posters covered many different aspects of the war. James Montgomery Flagg contributed the now famous "Uncle Sam Wants You!" poster. Wallace Morgan drew "Feed a Fighter" which promoted the victory garden. Charles Livingston Bull did the poster "Keep Him Free," urging Americans to buy war saving stamps. Harrison Fisher supported the Red Cross drive with his poster design. W.T. Benda got publicity for the Y.W.C.A. with his "Stand Behind the Country's Girlhood" poster. Joseph Pennell, who wanted to cover the war as an on-the-spot correspondent, found that he could not take the rigorous life at the battle front. He turned instead to publicizing the efforts of those who worked in the factories and shipyards back home. Altogether the Division of Pictorial Publicity contributed seven hundred poster designs, two hundred and eighty-seven cartoons, and four hundred and thirty-two cards and newspaper advertisements.

The United States Navy had its own division of publicity as part of the U.S. Navy Recruiting Bureau. Illustrator Henry Reuterdahl, a first lieutenant in the Navy, was its artistic advisor. He contacted fifty of his artist friends and personally urged them to help the Navy recruitment. George Wright, Albert Sterner, and James Daugherty, among others, responded with poster designs. Illustrators also served as advisors to the Navy on camouflaging techniques. The Marine Corps had an independent agency to deal with publicity but co-operated with the Division of Pictorial Publicity as well.

The Liberty Loan Committee in New York sponsored an unusual art exhibition for the war effort. In October of 1918, Fifth Avenue was turned into an exhibition hall. About one hundred stores and shops volunteered their windows as display cases for American art relating to the war. The Liberty Loan Committee also arranged for several artists to paint pictures in front of the New York Public Library. A large eight by sixteen foot frame was hung in front of the library and for twenty-two consecutive days, twenty-two artists painted pictures of the allied countries fighting World War One. Among the artists who participated were: James Montgomery Flagg,

[Trenches of World War One]
Raymond Sisley • Cat. no. 130

Henry Reuterdahl, F. Luis Mora, George Wright, Charles B. Falls, Adolph Treidler, W.T. Benda, William Glackens, and Charles Dana Gibson.

In May of 1917, Major Banning recommended to the Division of Pictures of the Committee on Public Information that artists be sent to France to keep official records of the action. He consulted Charles Dana Gibson regarding which artists should be sent. Eight men were chosen to be the official artists and they were commissioned to serve with the Engineer Reserve Corps. J. André Smith was the first of the group to be sent, followed by Ernest Peixotto, William James Aylward, Harry Townsend, Wallace Morgan, George Harding, Walter J. Duncan, and Harvey Dunn.

The orders to the men were as follows:

1. You are hereby directed to commence your work as official artist for the American Expeditionary Forces.
2. You are authorized to make sketches and paintings anywhere within the zone of the American Army in accordance with instructions already given you.
3. It is the wish of the Commander-in-Chief that all commanding officers extend to you all possible assistance in the carrying out of your orders.[2]

These orders gave the artists a very free hand in illustrating the war. Each man developed his own preferences for subject matter and methods of following the action. Smith's pictures were primarily landscapes of the European battlesites. Harvey Dunn invented a device whereby he could carry large sheets of paper on rollers to the front lines. He produced a few excellent drawings, but not the numbers produced by Peixotto, Harding, and Morgan. Arrangements were made for the artists to turn over their work the first day of each month so it could be forwarded to Washington. This meant that artists worked long, hard hours. They had to gather the material in their sketch books at the battle front and then in their spare time rework it, adding the detail and background.

Captain George Harding described the job in an article written after the war:

After a week with the advance, one's power of observation dulled, your head, your sketch book were filled with impressions; weak and weary and footsore one returned to the working billet — in my case a little French kitchen twelve by sixteen feet. Two drawings a day of the effects that impressed one the most was the working gait. In five or six days, having straightened out one's quick sketches, kept an eager eye on the happenings at the front, the fear of missing something drove one back to the fighting line, each trip always adding material, always learning something by experience, and always plunging in full enthusiasm, and coming out with a realization of inadequacy, that one was not artist enough to get it. It was not [a] place for preconceived ideas, for old receipts: what was needed was a clear vision of the new, an expression of power and elemental force as simple, in an entirely different way, as Winslow Homer's Maine Coast, or of the effects as simply put as a Hokusai drawing.[3]

By December of 1918, the overseas artists had returned one hundred and ninety-six drawings. An exhibition of this work opened in Washington D.C. and travelled to New York, Pittsburgh, and other cities around the country. The subject matter covered the full range of the war.

The official artists were not only ones sending back pictures. Magazine artists had been sent to the front as well. Periodicals not only carried news of the war but fictional stories of the "doughboys" in action. Will Foster wrote and illustrated "A Day with a Sketch Book at the Front," published by Scribner's in 1919. Raymond Sisley drew illustrations from his experiences with the 149th Artillery. Peixotto wrote a book which he illustrated from his war sketches called *The American Front* (1919). The American public was particularly interested in seeing the new technology of war, such as airplanes and machine guns. The violence and destruction, which was more devastating in this war than any before, was even more poignant with dramatic pictures to accompany texts.

NOTES

1. "Artist Who Never Saw a Battle Paints Noted War Pictures" from Boston Public Library artist clipping file, "YOHN," unidentified newspaper, December 17, 1927.
2. George Harding, "The American Artist at the Front," *The American Magazine of Art*, vol. 10 (1919), p. 453.
3. Harding, p. 453.

THE SPORTING LIFE

e-e-e-ow! Take another, Tommy! Slide! Sli-i-i-de! All right, I'll get 'em together after the game. Ain't this some game?

Edward Speya, "The Game and the Strike"

"Ye-e-e-e-ow! Take another, Tommy! Slide! Sli-i-i-de!..."
Arthur Ernest Becher • Cat. no. 9

lmost nothing seemed more important to Americans between 1890 and 1920 than pursuing the sporting life — except, perhaps, watching others pursue it and then reading about the outcome in the newspaper. Illustrations in newspapers focused increasing popular attention on sports and introduced new games to the American public.

The sporting life had been the subject of illustrations in America since the eighteenth century. In 1793, the *Massachusetts Magazine* published an engraving of a cricket game played at Dartmouth. *The Art of Swimming* was published in New York in 1818, with several plates showing the proper method of swimming. Even early children's books promoted such amusements as shuttlecock and battledore, leapfrog and skip-rope. Americans played many sports and games in the nineteenth century, but they were considered merely a pastime for the local community. In the 1840s, a few newspapers experimented with publishing the scores of local ball games in an attempt to build their circulations. The idea caught on, but it was not until the 1880s that the sports page emerged. The evolution of sports as public events and newspaper coverage went hand in hand. The more coverage a game received, the more popular it became in America.

"The End of the Century"
Arthur Burdett Frost • Cat. no. 62

Other factors besides the newspaper sports page influenced the development of organized sports in America in the decades between 1890 and 1920. Shorter working hours gave Americans more leisure time. Improvements in public transportation made it easier for people to get to sporting events. By the 1890s, Americans were enjoying such events as: the Kentucky Derby, professional baseball games, lawn tennis, American-style football, basketball, ice hockey, boxing, polo, and golf. Newspapers in these three decades not only covered the games, but also sent artists and photographers to capture the excitement for an eager public. In 1896, the first modern Olympics were held in Athens. America sent a team, but few people knew anything about the athletes until Americans began winning events. In 1900, the Olympics were held in Paris, followed at four-year intervals in St. Louis, London, Stockholm, and Antwerp. The first winter Olympics were held in Chamonix, France in 1924. Newspapers and periodicals sent photographers and artists to the games.

Because magazines were published weekly or monthly, they were less likely to cover the play-by-play aspects of a game. Instead, periodicals profiled a particular game or sports hero. They also capitalized on the popularity of sports by including fictional stories centred around sporting activities.

Some of the games were new to Americans, such as basketball and golf. In 1891, for example, the *New York Times* tried to explain what golfers did by describing the new craze as hitting white, hard-rubber balls with golf clubs into tin cups. Any explanation was meaningless without an actual picture of a golfer. In the same year, Canadian born Dr. James Naismith placed peach baskets at either end of a gymnasium and explained to eighteen boys in Springfield, Massachusetts that the object of basketball was to throw a soccer ball into the basket. Again, Americans needed both pictures and explanations before the game caught on.

A major controversy at the turn of the century concerned women's involvement in sports. There was a general belief that the sporting life was for men and women's exercise should be done privately and less vigorously. The tight corsets and long skirts worn by women prohibited any rigorous physical activity. Therefore, women who participated in fencing, baseball, basketball, and even football, wore bloomers, full blouses, stockings and flat shoes. The "immodesty" of these outfits outraged many people, and those women who continued to play sports were constantly ridiculed by the public. Ultimately, it was the sporting life that was largely responsible for the new freedom women experienced by looser clothes, shorter hemlines, and a healthier attitude towards their bodies.

Probably the most significant sporting refinement of these three decades was the bicycle. The bicycle had been around since the mid-nineteenth century, but as a heavy, awkward velocipede. Improvements in design made the bicycle lighter and the frame lower. This new bicycle was so popular with men and women that a fad swept the nation. By 1893, a million Americans were riding bicycles. Singers and actresses posed for publicity pictures on their bicycles. Charles Dana Gibson's already famous "Gibson Girl" took up cycling as an indication of her independent spirit. Arthur Burdett Frost illustrated several double-page spreads for *Harper's Weekly* of young people on bicycling expeditions (cat. no. 62). The fad lasted until 1900.

The sporting life among the upper class in America differed from the middle and lower classes, but the magazine-reading public was always eager to follow the comings and goings of such families as the Vanderbilts, the Astors, and the Van Rensselaers. Upper class Americans pursued yachting, polo, dressage, horse shows, and automobile motoring; and the reading public followed their play in the society pages of newspapers and magazines. *Vogue*, for example, reported regularly on the golf matches of the country club set and *Scribner's* did a series of little books on the summer activities of such resorts as Lenox, Massachusetts; Tuxedo, New York; and Bar Harbor, Maine.

FARAWAY PLACES

till better, we like to travel, to journey and sojourn in far countries, and amidst the outer strangeness to get more intimately at our inner selves. If we are novelists, we like to take our characters abroad, as if the home sparsity were not enough, and in resulting isolation to penetrate the last recesses of their mystery...

William Dean Howells

"A Bride of the Desert"
Irving Ramsay Wiles • Cat. no. 145

115

anderlust was something new to Americans at the turn of the century. No longer content to stay at home, they eagerly took long journeys abroad. Two factors influenced this trend. First, the Spanish-American War opened up discussions of international alliances and territorial expansion of the United States. Americans were ending a long period of isolationism and developing a new awareness of America and its relationship to the world. Secondly, transportation improved dramatically in the three decades from 1890 to 1920. In the 1890s, the horse and carriage dominated the streets and roads of the country. But by 1900, they were beginning to be phased out by the horseless carriage or automobile. Trains linked the nation for domestic travel, and trans-Atlantic ocean lines connected North America with Europe.

[Dock in a foreign port]
George Matthews Harding • Cat. no. 76

Since long journeys were expensive most Americans had to settle for armchair travelling in the pages of their favourite periodicals and parlour-table books. Publishers were very aware of the popularity of the travel pieces in their magazines. They spent large sums of money to send authors and illustrators on world-wide excursions. Author Julian Street, for example, teamed up with illustrator Wallace Morgan. The two men travelled together throughout the United States to do a series of articles for *Collier's* called "Abroad at Home." Morgan drew fifty-two sketches that accompanied Street's stories. Street had respect for illustrators and commented that when travelling with artists such as Morgan or May Wilson Preston, it was often the artist who pointed out details of local colour and interest he might otherwise have missed.

It was the sea that held allure for William James Aylward. *Scribner's, Harper's,* and *Collier's* (cat. no. 5) each published series centred around the artist's travels. "Unloading Christmas Trees," a double-page spread from *Collier's* is a good example of how the artist visualized images of the sea and ships.

Many noted illustrators were attracted to European scenery. Joseph Pennell, for example, did a series on French cathedrals; Jules Guérin drew French chateaux. Both of these series appeared in *Century*. George Wharton Edwards also chose to visit and paint Europe. His most famous pictorial essays were of Alsace-Lorraine, Belgium, Brittany, and Holland (cat. no. 51). Edwards looked for the picturesque landscapes of Europe and the faces and characters of the people. Ernest Peixotto also published pictures of his European travels (cat. no. 110). In 1906, he published a book of Italian scenery, and three years later, one on the French countryside. Peixotto then turned his attention to American scenery and illustrated travel books on California and the Southwest. Peixotto returned to Europe during World War One as an official war artist.

In 1921, the French government appointed him director of an American art school at Fontainebleau,and in 1922, he published another travel book on the landscapes of Spain and Portugal.

Publishers discovered a saleable feature by commissioning famous authors to do books about their travels. Henry James wrote *A Little Tour of France* (1884), illustrated by Joseph Pennell, and William Dean Howells wrote *Italian Journeys* (1872), which was revised in 1900 with the addition of Joseph Pennell's illustrations. A very elegant travel book was produced by the team of Edith Wharton and Maxfield Parrish. *Italian Villas and their Gardens* (1903), began as a series of articles for *Century*, and Wharton and Parrish were sent separately to Italy to do research and make sketches. They met after their trips to compare notes. When the articles began to appear, *Century* was very pleased with Parrish's illustrations, and it asked Wharton if she could make the text more lighthearted to suit the illustrations. Wharton was a serious landscape architect in her own right and considered these essays an important contribution to her field of interest. When she refused, and offered to drop out of the project, the editor backed down and the articles ran as they were.

More exotic locations were sought out by many illustrators. Irving Ramsay Wiles, for example, took his armchair-travellers to Arabia, capturing the bright desert light in his wash drawing of an Arabian bride (cat. no. 145). George Harding took his readers to the tropics in a large charcoal drawing depicting a ship in a foreign port (cat. no. 76). Malcolm Fraser, with the realism of a photographer, rendered the peoples of Mongolia for *Century Magazine* (cat. no. 59). It was unlikely that most Americans would ever visit such places, but books and periodicals allowed them to vicariously experience the world around them.

EPILOGUE

raphic imagery had never before been as pervasive nor as various as it was in the years 1890 to 1925. A popular visual culture emerged from this imagery. No longer did the written word dominate fashion, news, and entertainment. Pictures revealed the latest trends, they enlivened current events, they unfurled the scenery of the country, and the world, and they depicted attitudes, ideas and impressions of America at the turn of the century. But beyond being vivid representations, graphic images had the potency to create impressions, innovate ideas, and influence attitudes. The public looked at pictures in magazines, books, advertisements, and on posters. They also bought reproductions for their homes, hung them on the walls, and assimilated their contents on a daily basis. It was these images that influenced such American habits and behaviour, as the urge to consume and seek adventure.

In addition to the illustrations being a study of the influence on the contemporary public, they are an excellent record of the social history of the United States. Through pictures, historians are able to trace and study that history by analysing the tone and sentiment of the graphic imagery. When interpreted with the written word, illustrations communicate popular attitudes and outlooks of the era. Indeed, as documents of history, magazine and book illustrations are direct observations of important historic events as well as records of the lives of ordinary people.

Book and periodical illustration is also an important aspect in the development of the arts in America. Illustrator art was rarely experimental or avant-garde. It was rooted in the objective, realistic aesthetic on which American art was based before the second decade of the twentieth century. The art critiques of the Armory Exhibition of 1913 reveal how modern art shocked the majority of Americans who were used to traditional art. Illustration was seen by many as the "salvation" of the arts in America. Art critic, Thomas Craven, stated his idea of the role of illustration:

> The cult of modernism, in the beginning legitimately directed against photographic representation, has terminated in a denial of objective values and scattered the seeds of a 'pure and unadulterated art.' Such a notion has not only robbed painting of its fundamental interest in radical subject-matter but has left us with a large number of well-trained, and sufficiently talented, but utterly useless artists. I suggest that these lost souls turn their attention to illustration in the largest sense of the word — that they get acquainted with American life, and instead of promoting the 'aesthetic emotion' set down their experiences on canvas and give us new commentaries on the evolution of our national sense.[1]

Like so many remnants of the nineteenth century, illustration served as a buffer to the modern art of the twentieth century.

Lastly, illustration is an important adjunct to the study of literature in America. The styles and types of imagery which developed in book illustration followed the literary trends of the day. In the 1890s, the sentimental novel was at its zenith, followed by the semi-realists, the realists, and the naturalists. Illustrators visually interpreted these literary trends. Authors became increasingly aware of the potential for illustrations to set the mood and tone of their works. Mark Twain, for example, deliberately chose E.W. Kemble to illustrate the *Adventures of Huckleberry Finn* (1884), because he recognized that Kemble's graphic sense of humour would mitigate the controversial elements of the book.

The years 1890 to 1925 represent a time of optimism in America — a time when a philosophy of progress and expansionism prevailed. It was also a crucial period of cultural transformation. The visual contrasts of the era were dramatic. Cities sprang up where there had been open fields. Brownstones made way for towering skyscrapers. The horse and buggy were easily overpowered by the automobile. And the lacey Victorian dress looked old-fashioned beside the flapper's frock. The graphic imagery of American illustrators in this thirty-five year period encompassed the waning of an age of innocence and the beginning of a new, modern era.

NOTES

1. Thomas Craven, "The Decline of Illustration," *American Mercury*, vol. 12 (Oct. 1927), p. 207.

"To me he was great, a stranger, as some infant who born centuries ago..."
Denman Fink • Cat. no. 54

BIOGRAPHIES

KARL ANDERSON

Born Oxford, Ohio, 1874. Anderson began a career as a harness maker, but discovered his artistic talent in a job retouching photographs. He studied at the Académie Colarossi in Paris, and in Holland, Spain, and Italy. Anderson was also a pupil at the American Institute of Architects. He is well-known for his representation of the American beauty, often called the "Anderson Girl." Much of his career was centred in New York City, although he later made his home in Westport, Connecticut. His brother was the established American writer Sherwood Anderson. *Ladies' Home Journal, Saturday Evening Post, Everybody's,* and *Collier's* published many of Anderson's drawings. Two good examples of his work are found in *Journey's End* by Justus Miles Forman (New York, 1903) and *Iole* by Robert Chambers (New York, 1905). Anderson died in 1956.
(See cat. nos. 1 and 2)

EDMUND MARION ASHE

Born New York City, 1867. Ashe studied art under John Warde Stinson. During Theodore Roosevelt's administration, he was the White House artist-correspondent. One of the co-founders of the Silvermine Guild in Norwalk, Connecticut, Ashe taught at the Art Students' League in New York and the Carnegie Institute of Technology. Some of his best-known illustrations were for *In Camp with a Tin Soldier* (New York, 1892) by John Kendrick Bangs; *Her First Appearance* (New York, 1901), *Ransom's Folly* (New York, 1902), and *The Bar Sinister* (New York, 1903) by Richard Harding Davis. His drawings were also published in *St. Nicholas Magazine, Collier's, Scribner's Magazine,* and *Harper's Monthly.* His home was in Westport, Connecticut. Ashe died in 1941.
(See cat. no. 3)

WILLIAM JAMES AYLWARD

Born Milwaukee, Wisconsin, 1875. Aylward studied at the Art Institute of Chicago, the Art Students' League in New York, Howard Pyle's school in Chadds Ford, Pennsylvania, and privately in Europe. Images of the sea and ships were Aylward's speciality; an interest he developed in childhood as the son of a ship builder.

Scribner's commissioned Aylward to illustrate a trip around the world for a series of articles called "Sea Voyages of a Drydock" published in *Scribner's Magazine* in 1907. His periodical illustrations can also be found in *The American Magazine, Century, Collier's, Cosmopolitan, Country Gentleman, Delineator, Redbook, Harper's Monthly, Outing, Saturday Evening Post,* and *Ladies' Home Journal.* Famous books Aylward illustrated included: *Twenty Thousand Leagues Under the Sea* (New York, 1925) by Jules Verne, and *Sea Wolf* (New York, 1904) by Jack London. He was one of eight official artists of the American Expeditionary Force during World War One. In his later years Aylward taught at the Pratt Institute in Brooklyn, New York, and the Newark Public School of Fine and Industrial Art in New Jersey. He kept a studio in New York City for many years. His last known residence was in Washington, New York. Aylward died in 1956.
(See cat nos. 4 and 5)

GEORGE WATSON BARRATT

Born Salt Lake City, Utah, 1884. Barratt was a pupil of Robert Henri, William M. Chase, Edward Penfield, Luis Mora, and Howard Pyle. He sold his first drawing to *Women's Home Companion* and did advertising art for a short period. Art Young, a cartoonist with *Life,* saw Barratt's work and convinced him he was too good to limit himself to ad art alone. Through Young's influence, Barratt became one of the popular artists at *Life.* He was an active member of the Society of Illustrators and organized fund-raising events which led to the purchase of the current Society of Illustrators Building in New York City. Barratt is probably best remembered for his work in the theatre. He worked for the Ziegfield Follies from 1918 to 1934, was art director for the St. Louis Municipal Opera, and set designer for the Shubert Theatre. His illustrations appeared regularly in *Saturday Evening Post, Harper's Bazar, Life, Harper's Monthly,* and *Good Housekeeping.* During the years Barratt concentrated on illustration, he kept a studio in New York City. He died in 1962.
(See cat. no. 6)

EDWIN F. BAYHA

Very little is known about Bayha. He worked for *St. Nicholas Magazine* and *Harper's Weekly*. An example of Bayha's book illustration is found in Alfred T. Sheppard's *Running Horse Inn* (Philadelphia, 1907). He was a fellow at the Pennsylvania Academy of the Fine Arts. He lived in Glenside, Pennsylvania.
(See cat no. 7)

ARTHUR ERNEST BECHER

Born Freiberg, Germany, 1877. Becher moved to Milwaukee with his parents in 1885. His first art-related job was in a lithography shop. Becher attended a drawing class taught by Louis Mayer. Among the other young students in the class were William Aylward and Herman Pfeifer. Becher and Aylward studied under Howard Pyle in the fall of 1902, and moved to New York the following spring. In 1904, Becher married and settled in Ardsley, New York. While on assignment with *Appleton's Magazine* in Europe, he studied with Leopold O. Strutzel in Munich. Much of Becher's work was published by *Collier's, St. Nicholas Magazine, American Magazine, Century, Good Housekeeping, Harper's Monthly, Ladies' Home Journal, Youth's Companion, Saturday Evening Post, Redbook,* and *Woman's Home Companion.* Later in his career he concentrated on illustrations for novels. He moved to Fishkill, New York around 1916, but spent time in Arizona in the 1930s painting landscapes. Becher died in 1960.
(See cat. nos. 8 and 9)

WLADYSLAW THEODOR BENDA

Born Poznań, Poland, 1873. Benda attended the Krakow College of Technology and Art. He also studied in Vienna before moving to New York City in 1900. A few of Benda's better-known illustrations included: Frances Hodgeson Burnett's *The Little Hunchback Zia* (New York, 1916); Francis Marion Crawford's *The Little City of Hope* (New York, 1907); and Louise S. Houghton's *Russian Grandmother's Wonder Tales* (New York, 1906). Many of the leading periodicals such as *Sunday Magazine, McClure's Magazine, St. Nicholas Magazine, Scribner's Magazine, Cosmopolitan,* and *Everybody's* published his drawings. He is also remembered for his theatrical designs, especially for his "Benda Masks." Many of his best drawings were donated to the Library of Congress. He died in 1948.
(See cat. no. 10)

GERRIT ALBERTUS BÉNEKER

Born Grand Rapids, Michigan, 1882. Béneker studied at the Art Students' League in New York, the Art Institute of Chicago and privately under teachers Charles W. Hawthorne, John Vanderpoel, Frederick Richardson, and Henry Reuterdahl. Béneker lived for a short period in Arlington, New Jersey, but eventually made his home in Wellfleet, Massachusetts. He is remembered as a poet, etcher, painter, illustrator, and lecturer. Béneker believed that art was a means of communication between labourers, management, and the public. He worked in the Hydraulic Pressed Steel Company of Cleveland painting pictures which illustrated his premise. This formed the basis for an exhibition that was so popular it toured the United States for thirteen years. During World War One, Béneker illustrated a popular war poster which read "Sure, We'll finish the Job," celebrating the role of labour in winning the war. *Success* and *Everybody's* were two periodicals that published his drawings. Béneker died in Truro, Massachusetts in 1934.
(See cat. no. 11)

MARJORIE TORRE AND T.M. BEVANS

Very little is known about this married couple which signed their work merely "Bevans." They belonged to the Society of Illustrators in New York and many of their illustrations appeared in children's books and *St. Nicholas Magazine.* They also illustrated fashions for *Harper's Bazar* and *Ladies' Home Journal.*
(See cat. no. 12)

HANSON BOOTH

Born Noblesville, Indiana, 1885. Booth studied under the artists Vanderpoel and Bridgman. His brother Franklin was also an illustrator. Many of Hanson Booth's illustrations appeared in advertisements and educational textbooks. He also sold drawings to *Redbook, Success, Life, Everybody's,* and *Harper's Monthly.* He lived in New York City and Woodstock, New York. Booth died in Albany, California in 1944.
(See cat. nos. 14 and 15)

ARMAND BOTH

Born Portland, Maine, 1881. Both studied under Albert E. Moore and Eric Pape in Boston, and under Laurens and Steinlen in Paris. He was both an illustrator and a painter, and had a keen interest in dogs and fishing. He is noted for his creation of the American beauty, the "Both Girl." Mrs. Vernon Castle claimed it was modelled after her. His work appeared in *Collier's, St. Nicholas Magazine, Everybody's* and *Ladies' Home Journal.* He died in New Rochelle, New York in 1922.
(See cat. no. 16 and 17)

MAURICE L. BOWER

Born Ohio, 1889. Bower studied at the School of Industrial Art in Philadelphia under Walter Everett and then at Howard Pyle's Brandywine school in Chadd's Ford, Pennsylvania. Children's illustrations were a specialty with Bower, and he often recreated the romance of medieval times. Frances Hodgeson Burnett's *The Lost Prince* (New York, 1915) was among his best work. *St. Nicholas Magazine* and *Hearst* published his drawings. He lived most of his life in Philadelphia. Bower died in 1980.
(See cat. nos. 18 and 19)

M. LEONE BRACKER

Born Cleveland, Ohio, 1895. Bracker is remembered as one of the artists who provided designs for World War One posters. Among the works he illustrated was Francis Marion Crawford's *Wandering Ghosts* (New York, 1911). Bracker also worked as an advertising artist for many leading American manufacturers. He was one of the illustrators who created the advertising images for the Cream of Wheat Company. He also sold drawings to *The American Magazine* and *Good Housekeeping.* Bracker died in Rye, New Hampshire, in 1937.
(See cat. nos. 20 and 21)

PAUL BRANSOM

Born Washington, D.C., 1885. Bransom left school at fourteen and taught himself the basics of drawing. His first illustration assignment was with the *New International Encyclopedia.* He then took over Gus Dirk's comic strip, "News from Bugsville." Bransom had a love for animals and spent his spare time sketching at the zoo. Walt Kuhn saw his talent for drawing animals and encouraged him to paint. *Outing, Cosmopolitan, Saturday Evening Post,* and *St. Nicholas Magazine* published his drawings. Bransom's most memorable books all involve animal life, among them, Jack London's *Call of the Wild* (New York, 1912), and C.G.D. Roberts' *Children of the Wild* (New York, 1913). Bransom lived for a while in an artist-author colony in the Adirondacks, where illustrator Charles Sarka was among his friends. In later life he taught at the Jackson Hole, Wyoming, Teton Artists' Association. Bransom died in Quakertown, Pennsylvania in 1979.
(See cat. nos. 22 and 23)

GEORGE BREHM

Born Anderson, Indiana, 1878. Brehm was the older brother of illustrator, Worth Brehm. He studied at the Art Students' League in New York under Twachtman, DuMond, and Bridgman. *Delineator, Saturday Evening Post, Reader's Digest, Collier's, Ladies' Home Journal,* and other periodicals published his drawings. Brehm worked as an advertisting artist for several companies, among them the Colgate Company. He died in 1966.
(See cat. no. 24)

WORTH BREHM

Born Anderson, Indiana, 1883. Brehm studied at the John Herron Art Institute in Indianapolis, the Art Institute of Chicago, and the Art Students' League in New York. *Outing* published his first illustration. This led the way to illustration assignments with *Cosmopolitan, Good Housekeeping, Saturday Evening Post, Collier's,* and other magazines. Brehm is associated with the illustrations for books by two great American authors — Booth Tarkington's *Penrod and Sam* (Garden City, 1916); and Mark Twain's *The Adventures of Huckleberry Finn* (New York, 1923) and *The Adventures of Tom Sawyer* (New York, 1920). He died in Norwalk, Connecticut, in 1928.
(See cat. no. 25)

ARTHUR WILLIAM BROWN

Born Hamilton, Ontario, 1881. Brown studied at the Art Students' League in New York under: Frank Vincent DuMond, H. Siddon Mowbray, Kenyon Fox, F.R. Gruger and Walter Appleton Clark. He was active in the Society of Illustrators and served as its president from 1945 to 1947. His nickname among his fellow illustrators was "Brownie." A prolific draftsman, Brown illustrated for: *The Country Gentleman, Redbook, Ladies' Home Journal, Saturday Evening Post, Success,* and *Collier's.* Several noteworthy American authors were teamed with Brown, such as Booth Tarkington, F. Scott Fitzgerald, and O. Henry. He died in New York City in 1966.
(See cat. nos. 26, 27, and 28)

LEIGHTON BUDD

Budd was known primarily as a cartoonist and worked for the magazines *Puck, Life,* and *Scribner's Magazine.*
(See cat. no. 29)

CHARLES LIVINGSTON BULL

Born New York state, 1874. Bull worked first as a taxidermist's assistant at Ward's Museum in Rochester, New York. He received his formal art training at the Philadelphia Art School. Later, Bull worked as a taxidermist for the Natural History Museum in Washington, D.C. His drawing style was influenced by his friend and teacher, architect Harvey Ellis, who introduced Bull to Japanese prints and the Arts and Crafts Movement. Bull was most noted for his animal subjects demonstrated in the books he illustrated: *Under the Roof of the Jungle,* which he wrote; *Horsemen of the Plains* (New York, 1910) by Altsheler; and *Kindred of the Wild* (Boston, 1902) by C.G.D. Roberts. Bull died in Oradell, New Jersey in 1932.
(See cat. nos. 30 and 31)

JOHN HARMON CASSEL

Born Nebraska City, Nebraska, 1877. Cassel was a pupil at the Art Institute of Chicago. After 1911 he made his home in New York City. He was a cartoonist for the *Brooklyn Daily Eagle* as well as an illustrator for *American Legion Magazine, Liberty Magazine, Good Housekeeping,* and *St. Nicholas Magazine.* Many of Cassel's illustrations were humorous cartoonlike drawings satirizing American society. He was part of the Silvermine Artists' Guild in New Caanan, Connecticut. He held the position of cartoonist for the Brooklyn Daily Eagle. Cassel died in 1960.
(See cat. no. 32)

J. ANDRÉ CASTAIGNE

Born Angoulëme, France, 1861. Castaigne first studied in Paris, at the Académie Suisse, and later at the Ecole des Beaux Arts. Castaigne came to America in 1890. He became the director of the Charcoal Club in Baltimore, Maryland. Castaigne illustrated for *Ladies' Home Journal, Century, Harper's Weekly,* and *Scribner's Magazine.* A few of the well-known books he illustrated were: Thomas Nelson Page's *Polly* (New York, 1894) and *In Ole Virginia* (New York, 1896); Francis Marion Crawford's *Casa Braccio* (New York, 1895); Henry Cuyler Bunner's *Love in Old Clothes* (New York, 1896); Mary Catherwood's *Lazarre* (Indianapolis, 1901); and Silas Weir Mitchell's *The Guillotine Club* (New York, 1910). Castaigne was active until the 1930s.
(See cat. no. 33)

WILL COLBY

Colby was briefly associated with Howard Pyle at Pyle's school in Chadds Ford, Pennsylvania. Colby illustrated for: *Success, Redbook, Cosmopolitan,* and *Saturday Evening Post.* The later part of his life was spent in Arizona.
(See cat. no. 34)

SEWELL COLLINS

Born Denver, Colorado, 1876. Collins pursued a multiple career as illustrator-cartoonist and drama-critic-playwright. He received his art training at the Art Institute of Chicago from Herman McNeil. Collins was a cartoonist for the *Chicago Daily News*, a war correspondent for the *Chicago Tribune*, and a drama critic for the *New York Journal*. In 1904, he drew "The New American Girl," a poster design which was offered as a premium with the Armour Beef Extract Company. Collins moved to New York City in 1906, and accepted illustrating assignments from *Life, Collier's*, and *Munsey's*. Collins died in 1934.
(See cat. no. 35)

FANNY YOUNG CORY

Born Waukegan, Illinois, 1877. Cory studied first in Helena, Montana, and then moved to New York where she took classes at the Metropolitan School and the Art Students' League. She contributed regularly to *Century, Harper's Bazar, Ladies' Home Journal, Scribner's Magazine, Life, The Home Magazine, Saturday Evening Post, St. Nicholas Magazine*, and *McClure's Magazine*. Cory's first book illustration assignment was for Charles Battell Loomis' *Just Rhymes* (1899), which led to work with other leading authors, namely, Abbey Farwell Brown, Eva March Tappan, Josephine Dodge Daskam, Ellis Parker Butler, and L. Frank Baum. In 1903, she moved back to Canyon Ferry, Montana, and continued her illustrating career while raising a family. Cory wrote and illustrated three of her own books — all for children — called: *Sonny Sayings* (New York, 1929); *Little Miss Muffet* (Racine, 1936); and *Little Me* (New York, 1936). Cory died in Stanwood, Washington in 1972.
(See cat. no. 36)

PERCY ELTON COWEN

Born New Bedford, Massachusetts, 1883. Cowen studied at the Swain School of Design, the Eric Pape School in Boston, and the Art Students' League in New York. He illustrated for *Collier's, St. Nicholas Magazine, Century*, and *Everybody's* from 1909 to 1918. He kept a studio in New York City, but his home was in Chilmark, Martha's Vineyard, Massachusetts, where he died in 1923.
(See cat. no. 37)

PALMER COX

Born Granby, Quebec, 1840. Cox studied at the Granby Academy of Art, and later in San Francisco and New York. In 1875, he moved to New York where he worked for *Wild Oats*, a humorous weekly paper. Cox became famous in 1882 with the creation of "The Brownies." He drew these elfin creatures for *St. Nicholas Magazine*. Cox continued to draw them for the next thirty years and published several books about their adventures. Cox died in Granby, Quebec in 1924.
(See cat. nos. 38-43)

WILL CRAWFORD

Born Washington, D.C., 1869. Crawford studied briefly at art clubs in New York City and the surrounding area, but he was basically a self-taught artist. His style was characterized by shimmering light effects which he created by using white paper against a network of closely spaced lines. Crawford worked first for the New Jersey newspaper, *Newark Call*. Soon the *New York World* hired him as a staff artist. He shared a studio in New York with John Marchand and Albert Levering. Crawford's work appeared in *Life, Everybody's, Collier's, Munsey's, Cosmopolitan*, and *St. Nicholas Magazine*. He was one of the chief political cartoonists for *Puck* in the early 1900s. Crawford illustrated for authors: Owen Wister, Cyrus Townsend Brady, Ellis Parker Butler, Arthur Chapman, H.L. Mencken, and Theodore Roosevelt. Among his close friends were James Cagney, Will Rogers, and Frederic Remington. Crawford made his home in Jersey City, New Jersey. He died in Free Acres, New Jersey in 1944.
(See cat. no. 44)

MARGUERITE LOFFT DE ANGELI

Born Lapeer, Michigan, 1889. De Angeli was a self-taught artist. A neighbour, illustrator Maurice Bower, encouraged her artistic talents and secured assignments for her. Early in De Angeli's career she worked for *Ladies' Home Journal, St. Nicholas Magazine, Country Gentleman, The American Girl,* and *Women's Home Companion.* Authors she illustrated for included: Elizabeth Gray Vinney, Elizabeth Coalsworth, Cornelia Meigs, Tom Robinson, Eric Kelly, and Kathryn Worth. De Angeli wrote and illustrated two children's books — *The Book of Nursery and Mother Goose Rhymes* (Garden City, 1954) and *The Old Testament* (Garden City, 1966). She currently lives in Phildelphia.
(See cat no. 45)

CLYDE OSMER DE LAND

Born Union City, Pennsylvania, 1872. De Land studied music at the University of Rochester in Rochester, New York. He taught music and performed as a concert pianist before turning his attention to art. De Land attended Drexel Institute in Philadelphia and was one of Howard Pyle's prodigies at Chadds Ford, Pennsylvania. He is best known for his historical themes. Periodical illustrations by De Land can be found in *St. Nicholas Magazine, Cosmopolitan, Ladies' Home Journal,* and *Harper's Monthly.* He was a commercial artist for the American Telephone and Telegraph Company. Examples of De Land's book illustrations are found in John Bennett's *Barnaby Lee* (New York, 1902); Maud W. Goodwin's *White Aprons* (Boston, 1897); Charles Major's *A Forest Hearth: A Romance of Indiana* (New York, 1903); and Mrs. H.T. Comstock's *The Queen's Hostage* (Boston, 1906). Other authors De Land illustrated for were: Edmund Vance Cooke, Mary Catherine Crowley, William M. Graydon, Reginald Wright Kauffman, Lucy Foster Madison, and George R.R. Rivers. De Land's home was in Philadelphia. He died in 1947.
(See cat. no. 46)

HAROLD S. DE LAY

De Lay lived in Chicago, Illinois. Some of the books he illustrated were: Marguerite Bouvet's *The Smile of the Sphinx* (Chicago, 1911); William F. Frannan's *Thirty-one Years of the Plains and in the Mountains* (Chicago, 1908); William Edward Dubois' *The Quest of the Silver Fleece* (Chicago, 1911); Charles Pearce's *Love Besieged, a Romance of the Defense of Lucknow* (Chicago, 1911); and Drew Tuft's *Hiram Blair* (Chicago, 1912). De Lay's illustrations are also found in *St. Nicholas Magazine.*
(See cat. no. 47)

WALTER DE MARIS

Born Bridgeton, New Jersey, 1877. De Maris studied at the Art Students' League in New York. His illustrations appeared in *Saturday Evening Post, Woman's Home Companion, Munsey's, American Banker's Journal,* and in cheaper, pulp magazines. The Osbourne Company issued calendars using De Maris' illustrations. Three of the books he illustrated were: Comstock's *At the Crossroads* (New York, 1922); Mary E. and T.W. Hanshew's *The Riddle of the Mysterious Light* (New York, 1921); and Charles Norris Williamson's *The Brightener* (New York, 1921). De Maris died in New Rochelle, New York in 1947.
(See cat. no. 48)

WILLIAM WALLACE DENSLOW

Born Philadelphia, Pennsylvania, 1856. Denslow studied at the Cooper Union Art School and the National Academy of Design in New York. For two years he worked at the *Chicago Herald* before moving to San Francisco. In 1893, Denslow moved back to Chicago. He collaborated with author L. Frank Baum, illustrating *The Wonderful Wizard of Oz* (Chicago and New York, 1900). A disagreement split the Baum-Denslow team, and Denslow moved to an island in Bermuda. Financial problems plagued the later years of his life. He died in New York City in 1915.
(See cat. no. 49)

ARTHUR GARFIELD DOVE

Born Geneva, New York, 1880. Dove was taught to draw by a neighbour. From 1899 to 1901 he attended Hobart College, then transferred to Cornell University in Ithaca, New York, from which he graduated in 1903. He had a short-lived career in advertising in New York City. In 1908, he went to Europe to study painting. On Dove's return he settled in Westport, Connecticut where he earned his living by farming while he developed his painting career. He returned to illustrating about 1919. Dove contributed to *Success, McClure's Magazine, St. Nicholas Magazine, Collier's, Times, The American Boy, Life,* and *The Smart Set.* Dove is best remembered not for his illustrations, but for introducing abstract painting to America. He died in Huntington, New York in 1946. (See cat. no. 50)

GEORGE WHARTON EDWARDS

Born Fair Haven, Connecticut, 1869. Edwards studied painting in Antwerp and Paris. He began his career with the House of Harper as art editor Charles Parson's office boy. Edwards worked briefly in a printing house that made labels, and for a short period as a lithographer. He sold illustrations to *Century, St. Nicholas Magazine,* and *Scribner's Magazine.* From 1898 to 1903, he was director of *Collier's* Art Department and from 1904 to 1912 he was manager of the Art Department at the American Bank Note Company. Edwards travelled through Europe and was so impressed by the scenery, that he based many of his illustrations on it. He was well-known for illustrations which appeared in such books as: Mary Mapes Dodge's *Hans Brinker, or The Silver Skates* (New York, 1915); Hamilton Wright Mabie's *Book of Old English Ballads* (New York, 1903); Paul Leicester Ford's *A Checkered Love Affair* (New York, 1903); Oliver Wendal Holmes' *The Last Leaf* (Cambridge, 1886); and Bayard Taylor's *Home Ballads* (Boston, 1882). Edwards' own books included many pictorial essays of Europe. Noteworthy are: *Alsace-Lorraine* (Philadelphia, 1918); *Belgium Old and New* (Philadelphia, 1920); *Brittany and the Bretons* (New York, 1910); and *Holland of Today* (New York, 1909). Edwards made his home in Greenwich, Connecticut. He died in 1950. (See cat. no. 51)

ROBERT EDWARDS

Born Buffalo, New York, 1879. Edwards studied at the Art Students' League in Buffalo and New York, the Chase School, the Eric Pape School and the Cowles School in Boston. *Redbook, Saturday Evening Post, Everybody's,* and *Success* published his drawings. Examples of Edwards' book illustrations can be found in Mary Stewart Cutting's *Just for Two* (New York, 1909); Reginald Wright Kauffman's *Jarvis* (Boston, 1923); Alice MacGowan's *The Wiving of Lance Cleaverage* (New York, 1909); and William Bond Wheelwright's *A Harvard Alphabet* (New York, 1900). Edwards was also a landscape architect and a composer. He lived for several years in Beverly, Massachusetts. Edwards died in 1948. (See cat. no. 52)

WALTER HUNT EVERETT

Born Haddonfield, New Jersey, 1880. Everett attended Howard Pyle's classes in Chadds Ford, Pennsylvania. His illustrations appeared in *Harper's Monthly, Pictorial Review, Sunday Magazine, Ladies' Home Journal,* and *Saturday Evening Post.* He also illustrated such books as: Amelia Edith Barr's *The Hands of Compulsion* (New York, 1909); Cyrus Townsend Brady's *The Patriots; the Story of Lee and the Last Hope* (New York, 1912); D. Brinton Davis' *Trusia, A Princess of Krovitch* (1906); and George Hodges' *The Garden of Eden* (New York, 1909). Everett taught at the Pennsylvania Museum School of Industrial Art until 1914, and later at the Spring Garden Institute in Philadelphia. He kept a studio in Wilmington, Delaware through 1927. (See cat. no. 53)

DENMAN FINK

Born Springdale, Pennsylvania, 1880. Fink studied at the Pittsburgh School of Design, the Boston Museum of Fine Arts and the Art Students' League in New York. He was a muralist and architect as well as an illustrator. Fink was one of twenty-two artists who painted a mural for the Fourth Liberty Loan and United War Work Campaign. His illustrations appeared regularly in *Harper's, American Magazine, Saturday Evening Post, Collier's, Century, St. Nicholas Magazine,* and *Scribner's Magazine.* Authors Fink illustrated books for included: Rex Beach, Mary Austin, Katharine Loose, and George Merrick Mullett. He also did commercial illustrations for the Cream of Wheat Company. Fink was on the Art Department faculty at the University of Miami for twenty-five years. He died in Miami, Florida in 1956.
(See cat. no. 54)

BLANCHE V. FISHER [GREER]

Born Eldora, Iowa, 1884. Fisher was a pupil of William M. Chase and Eben F. Comins. She also studied under Guerin and Naudin in Paris. Her illustrations appeared in *Collier's, St. Nicholas Magazine, Harper's, Everybody's,* and *Saturday Evening Post.* Fisher's book illustration credits included: Joanna Spyri's *Eveli, The Little Singer* (Philadelphia, 1926) and Eleanor Sloan's *All Sorts of Good Stories* (New York, 1930). Scribner's hired Fisher to do textbook illustrations. She was also a painter, etcher and teacher. From 1933 to 1947 she lived in Summit, New Jersey.
(See cat. nos. 55 and 56)

HARRISON FISHER

Born Brooklyn, New York, 1875. Fisher studied art with his father, Hugo Fisher, and with Amedeé Joullin in San Francisco, and at Mark Hopkins Institute of Art. His first job was working for *Puck* in New York. Fisher is most noted for his creation of the "Fisher Girl," his version of the American beauty, which appeared regularly on the covers of *Cosmopolitan* for twenty-five years. He was one of the highest paid illustrators of this era. His illustrations are also found in *Saturday Evening Post, McClure's Magazine, Life, Ladies' Home Journal, Puck, Scribner's Magazine,* and *Century.* He illustrated the books of Paul Leister Ford, Harold Frederic, Bret

Harte, Elenor Hoyt Brainerd, George Barr McCutcheon, and Mary Roberts Rinehart. Fisher's own picture books featuring beautiful American women included: *A Dream of Fair Women* (Indianapolis, 1907); *The Harrison Fisher Book* (New York, 1907); *Bachelor Belles* (New York, 1908); *American Beauties* (Indianapolis, 1909); *Fair Americans* (New York, 1911); *Harrison Fisher's American Girls in Miniature* (New York, 1912); and *Harrison Fisher Girls* (New York, 1914). Fisher also designed several posters during World War One. He died in New York City in 1934.
(See cat. no. 57)

ERNEST GEORGE FOSBERY

Born Ottawa, Ontario, 1874. Fosbery studied under Franklin Brownell from 1890 to 1897. From 1897 to 1898 he studied under Fernand Cormon in Paris. Fosbery moved to Buffalo, New York in 1907 as headmaster of the Art Students' League. In 1911, he returned to Ottawa and taught at the Ottawa Art Association. Fosbery is remembered chiefly as a portrait painter. His illustration career was limited to his early years. His drawings were published in *Youth's Companion* and *Life.* An example of his book illustration is found in Stephen Conrad Stuntz's *The Second Mr. Jim* (Boston, 1904). Fosbery died in Cowansville, Quebec in 1960.
(See cat. no. 58)

MALCOLM FRASER

Born Montreal, Quebec, 1869. Fraser studied at the Académie Julian and Ecole des Beaux-Arts in Paris, and at the Art Student's League in New York under Kenyon Cox and Wyatt Eaton. Fraser contributed drawings to *Century, St. Nicholas Magazine, Ladies' Home Journal,* and other magazines. Popular books Fraser illustrated included: Mary Noailles Murfree's *The Young Mountaineers* (Boston and New York, 1897); F. Hopkinson Smith's *Caleb West, Master Driver* (Boston and New York, 1898); and several Bret Harte stories. Fraser died in Brookhaven, Long Island in 1949.
(See cat. no. 59)

ARTHUR BURDETT FROST

Born Philadelphia, Pennsylvania, 1851. Frost apprenticed to a wood engraver and then to a lithographer. He studied briefly at the Pennsylvania Academy of the Fine Arts under Thomas Eakins. In 1876, Frost joined the staff of *Harper's*. From 1906 to 1914 he lived in Europe. Frost returned to America and settled in Pasadena, California. P.F. Collier published a *Book of Drawings* by Frost in 1904. He is remembered for his humorous drawings, sporting illustrations, and depictions of country life. Teamed with author Joel Chandler Harris, Frost illustrated the unforgettable stories of American folklore, *Uncle Remus: His Songs and Sayings* (New York, 1895). Frost died in Pasadena, California in 1928.
(See cat. nos. 60, 61, and 62)

ERNEST FUHR

Born New York City, 1874. Fuhr was a pupil of William M. Chase and also studied in Paris. His first experience with illustrating was as a newspaper artist. Fuhr was influenced by the work of the Philadelphia Realists. He contributed regularly to *Saturday Evening Post, Everybody's, Youth's Companion, American Boy,* and *Collier's*. Examples of his book illustrations are found in Alexander Black's *Richard Gordon* (Boston, 1902); Owen McMahon Johnson's *Skippy Bedelle* (Boston, 1922); and Albert Kinross' *The Truth about Vignolles* (New York, 1922). Fuhr died in Westport, Connecticut in 1933. Much of his work was left to the Library of Congress, Washington, D.C.
(See cat. nos. 63 and 64)

GEORGE GIBBS

Born New Orleans, Louisianna, 1870. Gibbs studied at the Naval Academy for nearly three years, and later studied in Switzerland. He spent four years at the Art Students' League in New York before he moved to Washington, D.C. In Washington, Gibbs was a newspaper writer and sold real estate to support his art training at the Corcoran School of Art. At twenty-two, he moved to Phildelphia, and accepted a position as a staff artist with the *Saturday Evening Post*. Among the books he illustrated were: Richard Harding Davis' *The White Mice* (New York, 1904); Charles Heber Clark's *The Quakeress* (Philadelphia, 1905); Hornor Cotes' *The Counterpart* (New York, 1909); and Emma Payne Erskine's *The Eye of Dread*. Gibbs wrote and illustrated

his own book *Pike and Cutlass, Hero Tales of Our Navy* (Philadelphia, 1900). He was also a novelist and wrote fifty books in his lifetime as well as a dozen screenplays for films. Gibbs served as president of the Franklin Inn Club. He is best remembered as a painter and muralist. His son, T. Harrison Gibbs, was a noted sculptor. Gibbs' home was Rosemont, Pennsylvania. He died in 1942.
(See cat. no. 65)

JOSEPH J. GOULD

Born Philadelphia, Pennsylvania, c.1880. Gould studied at the Pennsylvania Academy of the Fine Arts from 1894 to 1895. He worked for *Holland's Magazine, Ladies' Home Journal, Saturday Evening Post, Success, Scribner's Magazine, Moods,* and *Footlights*. His book illustration credits included: Charles Newman Crewson's *Tales of the Road* (Chicago, 1905); Montagne M. Glass' *Abe and Mawruss* (New York, 1911); Booth Tarkington's *In the Arena, Stories of Political Life* (New York, 1905); and Charles Stokes Wayne's *The Sable Lorcha* (Chicago, 1912). Gould contributed an essay on illustration for the American Federation of Arts correspondence school. He also did advertisement artwork for the National Phonograph Company. Gould died in Philadelphia, c.1935.
(See cat. no. 66)

GORDON HOPE GRANT

Born San Francisco, California, 1875. Grant studied art in England at Heatherly and Lambeth. He returned to America and served on the Mexican border with the 7th Regiment of the National Guard. *Harper's* hired Grant as illustrator-correspondent during the Boer War. Nautical subjects were his specialty. Grant's illustrations appeared in such periodicals as: the *San Francisco Chronicle, The Examiner, Harper's, Puck,* among others. Chief among the books he illustrated were: Booth Tarkington's *Penrod* (Garden City, 1914); O. Henry's *Ransom of the Red Chief* (Garden City, 1918); and Henry Brundage Culver's *The Book of Old Ships* (New York, 1935). Grant also wrote and illustrated several books, including: *Story of the Ship* (New York, 1919); *Sail Ho!* (New York, 1931); and *Greasy Luck* (New York, 1932). His home was in New York City where he died in 1962.
(See cat. no. 67)

WALTER GRANVILLE-SMITH

Born South Granville, New York, 1870. Granville-Smith studied under Walter Satterlee, Carroll Beckwith, and Willard Metcalf. He attended classes at the Art Students' League in New York and travelled throughout Europe. His work appeared in many leading periodicals. He is remembered as the creator of many of the Proctor and Gamble Ivory Soap advertisements. His home was in New York City, but he also spent time in Bellport, Long Island. Granville-Smith died in 1938.
(See cat. no. 68)

ELIZABETH SHIPPEN GREEN [ELLIOTT]

Born Philadelphia, Pennsylvania, 1871. Green attended the Pennsylvania Academy of the Fine Arts, studying under Robert Vonnoh, Thomas Eakins, and Thomas Anshutz. Later she studied under Howard Pyle at the Drexel Institute in Philadelphia and then studied abroad for six years. Green began her career as an advertising illustrator and a newspaper artist, but later went under exclusive contract for *Harper's* from 1902 to 1911. Her work may also be found in *Ladies' Home Journal, Saturday Evening Post,* and *St. Nicholas Magazine.* Books she illustrated included: Charles Lamb's *Tales of Shakespeare* (Philadelphia, 1922) and Josephine Preston's *Book of the Little Past* (1908). Before her marriage to Hugar Elliott, she shared a studio with Jessie Willcox Smith and Violet Oakley, two prominent female illustrators. Green died in 1954.
(See cat. nos. 69 and 70)

DAN SAYRE GROESBECK

Born 1879. Groesbeck worked as an illustrator for *Liberty Magazine, Harper's Weekly, Everybody's, Collier's, Cosmopolitan, Century,* and *Success.* Examples of his book illustrations can be found in Henry James O'Brien Bedford-Jones' *Flamehair the Skuld* (Chicago, 1913); Harry Graham's *Missrepresentative Women* (New York, 1906); Jack London's *The Strength of the Strong* (Chicago, 1912); and Harry Lincoln Sayler's *The Blind Lion of the Congo* (Chicago, 1912); and *The King Bear of Kadiak Island* (Chicago, 1912). Groesbeck worked as a reporter and artist for a Los Angeles newspaper. He illustrated many of O. Henry's newspaper stories. Groesbeck was also a muralist, printmaker, and reporter-artist. His obituary states he was a soldier of fortune. Groesbeck died in Los Angeles in 1950.
(See cat. no. 71)

JAY HAMBIDGE

Born Simcoe, Ontario, 1867. Hambidge's first jobs were as a "printer's devil" for the *Kansas City Star* and staff artist for the *New York Herald.* He attended evening classes at the Art Students' League in New York studying under William M. Chase. Later he shared a studio with the noted illustrator Walter Appleton Clark. Hambidge's work appeared regularly in the pages of *Century, St. Nicholas Magazine, American Magazine, Success,* and *Collier's.* Noted books he illustrated were: Francis Lynde's *Empire Builders* (Indianapolis, 1907); Ida Tarbell's *He Knew Lincoln* (New York, 1907); Brand Whitlock's *The Turn of the Balance* (Indianapolis, 1907); and Albert Jay Nock's *What We All Stand For* (New York, 1913). Hambidge was also an art historian and author of *Dynamic Symmetry: The Greek Vase* (1920). He died in New York City in 1924.
(See cat. nos. 72, 73, and 74)

CHARLOTTE HARDING [BROWN]

Born Newark, New Jersey, 1873. Harding attended the Philadelphia School of Design for Women, the Pennsylvania Academy of the Fine Arts, the Drexel Institute in Philadelphia, and studied under Howard Pyle in Chadds Ford, Pennsylvania. Her works appeared in *American Magazine, Collier's, The Critic, Good Housekeeping, Harper's Monthly, Ladies' Home Journal, Saturday Evening Post,* and *Youth's Companion.* A prolific illustrator, Harding's drawings can be found in the books of authors: Eva March Tappan, Alice Duer Miller, Helen Way Whitney, Francis Neilson, Mary Raymond Andrews, and William Dean Howells. Harding died in Smithtown, Long Island in 1951.
(See cat. no. 75)

GEORGE MATTHEWS HARDING

Born Philadelphia, Pennsylvania, 1882. Harding was the younger brother of Charlotte Harding. He studied at the Pennsylvania Academy of the Fine Arts from 1899 to 1900 and later attended Howard Pyle's school at Chadds Ford, Pennsylvania. During World War One, Harding was a captain with the Army Engineers in Europe, assigned to record panoramas of battles. His focus in these drawings was on agony of war in individual lives. In World War Two he was an artist in the Marines. In 1906, Harding began his illustration career with *Harper's* and was assigned as a roving artist to do pictures in Newfoundland and Labrador. His drawings also appeared in *Collier's, Ladies' Home Journal, Liberty, Outing, McClure's Magazine, Delineator, Cosmopolitan, American Magazine,* and *Saturday Evening Post.* Later in life he taught at the Pennsylvania Academy of the Fine Arts and at the University of Pennsylvania. Harding is also remembered as a muralist. He died in Wynnewood, Pennsylvania in 1959.
(See cat. nos. 76 and 77)

HERMAN HEYER

Born Germany, 1876. Heyer's family immigrated to the United States when he was an infant. He studied art in Paris, returning to America to pursue a career in illustration with such magazines as: *Success, Collier's, Sunday Magazine, Hearst's, Munsey's,* and *Demarest.* Heyer's book illustration credits included: Margaret Sidney's *Five Little Peppers and How They Grew* (Boston, 1903); Robert Barr's *A Rock in the Baltic* (New York, 1906); George Eggleston's *Love is the Sum of It* (Boston, 1907); Arthur Charles Fox-Davis' *The Duplicate Death* (New York, 1910); Nina Larrey Duryea's *The House of the Seven Gabblers* (New York, 1911); and Mittie Owen McDavid's *The Children of the Meadows* (New York, 1912). Heyer was recognized as one of the creators of the American beauties. In later life he was chief artist for Paramount Pictures, Inc. He died in Bay Shore, Long Island in 1950.
(See cat. no. 78)

WILLIAM ELY HILL

Born Binghampton, New York, 1886. Hill graduated from Amherst College and studied art at the Art Students' League in New York. He is best remembered as a cartoonist. *Vanity Fair, Redbook, Everybody's, Puck, McClure's Magazine, American Magazine,* and *Life* published many of his humorous drawings. Hill was also featured as a cartoonist in the *New York Herald Tribune* with the series called "Among Us Mortals." He wrote and illustrated a book called *Among Us Cats* (New York, 1926). After a career of forty-four years in illustration, he retired in 1960. Hill died in Redding, Connecticut in 1962.
(See cat. no. 79)

LUCIUS WOLCOTT HITCHCOCK

Born West Williamsfield, Ohio, 1868. Hitchcock grew up in Akron, Ohio. He studied art at the Art Students' League in New York, and in Paris under Jules Lefebvre, Benjamin Constant, and Jean Paul Laurens. Hitchcock illustrated for *Scribner's Magazine, Redbook, Everybody's, Harper's, Collier's,* and *McClure's Magazine.* A few of the best-known books he illustrated were: Mark Twain's *A Double Barrelled Detective Story* (New York, 1902) and *A Horse's Tale* (New York, 1907); Margaret Wade Deland's *Dr. Lavendar's People* (New York, 1903); Alice French's *The Man of the Hour* (New York, 1905); Henry Wadsworth Longfellow's *The Courtship of Miles Standish* (Boston, 1888); Adele Leuhrmann's *The Other Brown* (New York, 1917); Julia Magruder's *Her Husband* (Boston, 1911); and Booth Tarkington's *The Conquest of Canaan* (New York, 1905). Hitchcock taught at the Buffalo Fine Arts Academy. He spent his summers in Southport, Maine and winters in New Rochelle, New York. He died in New Rochelle in 1942.
(See cat. no. 80)

ROBERT BRUCE HORSFALL

Born Clinton, Iowa, 1869. Horsfall studied at the Cincinnati Art Academy, the Royal Bavarian Academy, and at the Académie Colarossi in Paris. Animals were his primary subjects. In 1906, he worked at the American Museum of Natural History in New York, where he did the background drawings for habitat groups. Horsfall was also associated with the drawings for the Princeton Patagonian Report (1904-1914). His illustrations appeared in *Scribner's Magazine, Century,* and *St. Nicholas Magazine.* Horsfall illustrated some literary works for such popular artists as: Dallas Lore Sharpe, Egbert Chesley Allen, Willard A. Eliot, William B. Scott, and Eva Rodimer. He was the author of thirty nature books. Horsfall died in Red Bank, New Jersey in 1948.
(See cat. no. 81)

HENRY HUTT

Born Chicago, Illinois, 1875. Hutt studied briefly at the Art Institute of Chicago before moving to New York. *Life* published his first illustration which lead to a position as a commercial illustrator, and then to a position with an engraving and printing establishment. His works, which appeared in several leading periodicals, usually detailed the life of the "smart set." Creator of the "Hutt Girl," he was one of many illustrators to bring international attention to the American woman. He married one of the models for the "Hutt Girl," Edna Garfield Della Torre. Century published a book of his beautiful women in 1908 called *The Henry Hutt Picture Book.* Other pictures of "Hutt Girls" can be found in *Girls, by Henry Hutt* (New York, 1910); *Rosebuds* (Indianapolis, 1912); and *She Loves Me* (Indianapolis, 1911). Hutt also illustrated the romantic novels of Paul Leister Ford, Robert William Chambers, Emerson Hough, Gouverneur Morris, Grace Richmond, and Booth Tarkington. Hutt died in a fire-related accident in the Bronx, New York in 1950.
(See cat. no. 82)

WILLIAM LEROY JACOBS

Born Cleveland, Ohio, c.1869. Jacobs studied in Paris at Académie Julian and Académie Colarossi. His illustrations appeared in *Century, Harper's Weekly, Collier's, Delineator, Ladies' Home Journal, Cosmopolitan, Life,* and *St. Nicholas Magazine.* Books which Jacobs illustrated included: Thomas Nelson Page's *A Captured Santa Claus* (New York, 1902); Frank Luciens Parkard's *Greater Love Hath No Man* (New York, 1913); Gene Porter's *The Harvester* (Garden City, 1911); Elizabeth Waltz's *Pa Gladden* (New York, 1904); and Helen Smith Woodruff's *Mis' Beauty* (New York, 1911). He died in New York City in 1917.
(See cat. no. 83)

ARTHUR EDWARD JAMESON

Born United Kingdom, 1872. Jameson studied at the Art Students' League in New York. He worked for *Success, Life, Cosmopolitan,* and *Judge,* and also as a commercial illustrator for the G.W. Dillingham Company. A sample of his work can be found in Arthur Hornblow's *The End of the Game* (New York, 1907).
(See cat. no. 84)

MARTIN JUSTICE

Born 1892. Justice's illustrations can be found in *Century, Collier's,* and *Munsey's.* Books he illustrated included: Anna Alice Chapin's *The Under Trail* (Boston, 1912); William Tillinghast Eldridge's *Hilma* (New York, 1907); George Horace Lorimer's *Letters from a Self-Made Merchant to his Son* (Philadelphia, 1901); John Hartley Manners' *Peg O' My Heart* (New York, 1913); Harvey Jerrold O'Higgins' *Old Clinkers* (Boston, 1909); and David Potter's *I Fasten a Bracelet* (Philadelphia, 1911). Justice died in Hollywood in 1960.
(See cat nos. 85 and 86)

GERTRUDE ALICE KAY

Born Alliance, Ohio, 1884. Kay studied at the Philadelphia School of Design for Women and under Howard Pyle at his school in Chadds Ford, Pennsylvania. She contributed cover designs to *Ladies' Home Journal* in the 1920s and also illustrated for *St. Nicholas Magazine, Everybody's, Child Life, Country Gentleman, Good Housekeeping, McCalls', Woman's Home Companion,* and *Youth's Companion.* Her specialty was juvenile book illustration. Samples of her work can be found in Sarah Addington's *The Great Adventures of Mr. Claus* (Boston, 1923) and *Round the Year in Pudding Lane* (Boston, 1924); and Florence Bernard's *Through the Cloud Mountain with Gun...* (Philadelphia, 1922). Kay also wrote and illustrated four children's books — *When the Sand Man Comes* (New York, 1916); *The Book of Seven Wishes* (New York, 1917); *Helping the Weatherman* (New York, 1920); and *Us Kids and the Circus.* Kay died in Youngstown, Ohio in 1939. A bibliography of her works was assembled after her death by the Rodman Public Library in Alliance, Ohio.
(See cat. no. 87)

ARTHUR IGNATIUS KELLER

Born New York City, 1867. Keller studied at the National Academy of Design in New York, under Wilmarth and also under Loefftz in Munich. Keller was employed by the leading periodicals of his time, such as: *Delineator, Cosmopolitan, Collier's, McClure's Magazine, Scribner's Magazine, Harper's, Ladies' Home Journal, Sunday Magazine,* and *Century.* He collaborated with many of America's popular authors such as: Charles Wadsworth Camp, Maurice Francis Egan, Mary Eleanor Freeman, James Russell Lowell, Bret Harte, William Dean Howells, Francis Hopkinson Smith, Frank Stockton, Elizabeth Stuart Ward, Thomas Dixon, Kathleen Norris, and Louis Joseph Vance, as well as on new editions by famous authors such as: Charles Dickens, Nathaniel Hawthorne, and Washington Irving. Keller died in Riverdale, New York in 1924. His widow donated many of his best drawings to the Library of Congress in Washington, D.C. A retrospective of his work was organized by the Cragsmoor Public Library in New York in 1978.
(See cat. nos. 88 and 89)

ROLLIN KIRBY

Born Galva, Illinois, 1875. Kirby received his early art training in Nebraska. At age nineteen, he moved to New York and studied at the Art Students' League. He also studied under James MacNeill Whistler in Paris. Kirby's early illustrations appeared in *Collier's, Life, St. Nicholas Magazine,* and *McClure's Magazine,* but his real fame came from cartooning. He won the Pulitzer Prize three times for political cartoons which appeared in the *New York World, New York Post, New York Evening Mail,* and *New York Sun.* His illustrations also appeared in *Century, Good Housekeeping, American Magazine, Liberty,* and *Scribner's Magazine.* Kirby illustrated: Wallace Adman Irwin's *Letters of a Japanese Schoolboy* (New York, 1909); Walter Lippmann's *Men of Destiny* (New York, 1928); and Vance Thompson's *Spinners of Life* (Philadelphia, 1903). His own book was titled *High Lights, A Cartoon History of the Nineteen Twenties* (New York, 1931). Kirby lived most of his life in New York City, although summers were usually spent in Weston, Connecticut. He died in New York City in 1952.
(See cat. no. 90)

OTTO LANG

Lang worked for *Life* and *Sunday Magazine.* He died in 1940.
(See cat. no. 91)

GERALD LEAKE

Born London, England, 1885. Leake left London for New York City to pursue an illustration career. His works appeared in *Pictorical Review, St. Nicholas Magazine, Everybody's,* and *Century.* He was an associate of the National Academy of Design in New York. Examples of his book illustration are found in Mark Lee Luther's *The Boosters* (Indianapolis, 1924); Henry John Newbolt's *Taken from the Enemy* (London, 1911); and Vance Thompson's *The Pointed Tower* (Indianapolis, 1923). Leake died in 1975.
(See cat. no. 92)

WILLIAM ROBINSON LEIGH

Born Falling Waters, West Virginia, 1866. Leigh studied at the Maryland Institute in Baltimore, and then at the Royal Academy of Fine Arts in Munich where he studied under Raupp, Gysis, Loefftz, and Lindenschmid. He was in Munich for twelve years during which time he returned only once to the United States. His subject matter was usually the American West. Leigh's illustrations appeared in *Collier's* and *Scribner's Magazine*. From 1926 to 1927, and again in 1928, he participated in expeditions to East Africa. He painted the background for animal habitats for the American Museum of Natural History in New York. Leigh illustrated the works of authors Herbert Quick and Jesse Lynch. Two of his own books were: *The Western Pony* (New York, 1933) and *Frontier's of Enchantment* (New York, 1938). Leigh died in New York City in 1955.
(See cat. no. 93)

HARRY A. LINNELL

Born Attleboro, Massachusetts, 1873. Linnell studied under F.V. Du Mond, C. Bechwith, William M. Chase, and Luis Mora. He worked for: *Century, Sunday Magazine, St. Nicholas Magazine, Cosmopolitan, McClure's Magazine,* and *Life*. Linnell and Charlotte Harding illustrated Jean Webster's *Much Ado about Peter* (New York, 1909).
(See cat. no. 94)

JOHN NORVAL MARCHAND

Born Leavenworth, Kansas, 1875. Marchand was often referred to as "March." He was primarily a Western painter and illustrator. He illustrated the books of authors: Cyrus Townsend Brady, Hamlin Garland, Margaret Hill McCarter, Anna Maynard Barbour, David Belasco, Herbert Coolidge, Jackson Gregory, and Archie P. McKishnie. His works also appeared in *St. Nicholas Magazine* and *Century*. He resided most of his life in New York, but died in Westport, Conneticut in 1921.
(See cat. no. 95)

FRANK BIRD MASTERS

Born Watertown, Massachusetts, 1873. Masters studied first under C.H. Woodburg and then under Howard Pyle in 1903 and 1904. He illustrated for: *Success, Collier's, Ladies' Home Journal, Youth's Companion, St. Nicholas Magazine, Harper's Weekly, Cosmopolitan,* and *Everybody's*. Later in his career he had an exclusive contract with *Saturday Evening Post*. A few examples of his book illustrations can be found in James Jeffery Roche's *Her Majesty the King* (Boston, 1899); Francis Thorpe's *The Spoils of Empire* (1903); Samuel Merwin's *The Road-Builders* (New York, 1905); and William Nathaniel Harben's *Mam' Linda* (New York, 1907). Masters had his studio in New York City, and later in Brooklyn.
(See cat. nos. 96 and 97)

HARRY A. MATHES

Born 1882. Mathes is remembered as both a painter and illustrator. He worked for *Harper's* from 1905 to 1906. An example of Mathes' book illustration can be found in Emerson Hough's *The Lady and the Pirate* (Indianapolis, 1913). He died in New York in 1969.
(See cat. no. 98)

WALLACE MORGAN

Born New York, 1873. Morgan studied at the National Academy of Design in New York for six years. He began a career as a newspaper artist with the *New York Herald and Telegram* in 1898. During this period of employment with the paper he developed a quick, facile style. It was a skill that aided him his entire career. He filled sketchbooks with quick sketches that he later re-used, depending on the needs of a particular picture. Morgan was one of eight artists chosen to record the battles and scenes of World War One. He did illustrations for: *McClure's Magazine, Collier's, Cosmopolitan, The New Yorker, Saturday Evening Post,* and the *New York Times Magazine*. In 1914, he travelled with author Julian Street to research a series for *Collier's* called "Abroad at Home." It was so popular that in 1917 he and Street did another series called "American-Adventures." Morgan illustrated books for authors: Carolyn Wells, Richard Harding Davis, Christopher Morley, Joseph Lincoln, Norman Henry Crowell, Charles Belmont Davis, Myra Kelly, Grace Lockwood Roosevelt, Booth Tarkington, Charles H.

Towne, Edward W. Townsend, and Edward C. Wagenknecht. As a cartoonist Morgan created the memorable character "Fluffy Ruffles." He was also associated with art direction in the film industry. In later years he taught at the Art Students' League in New York. Morgan died in New York in 1948.
(See cat. nos. 99 and 100)

PETER SHEAF HERSEY NEWELL

Born McDonough County, Illinois, 1862. Newell studied briefly at the Art Students' League in New York, but was largely a self-taught artist. His illustrations appeared in *Harper's, St. Nicholas Magazine, Youth's Companion,* and *Scribner's Magazine.* He is most often associated with children's book illustration. Six of Newell's own books were quite popular. They were: *Topsys & Turveys* (New York, 1893); *Shadow Show* (New York, 1896); *Pictures and Rhymes* (New York, 1899); *The Hole Book* (New York, 1908); *The Slant Book* (New York, 1910), and *The Rocket Book* (New York, 1912). He also illustrated for authors: John Kendrick Bangs, Stephen Crane, Mary Eleanor Freeman, Frank Stockton, and Guy Wetmore Carryl. Newell died in Little Neck, New York in 1924.
(See cat. no. 101)

FLORENCE ENGLAND NOSWORTHY

Born Milwaukee, Wisconsin, 1872. Nosworthy was a pupil of Edmund Tarbell and Kenyon Cox. She attended the Boston Museum of Fine Arts School, the Cowles Art School, and the Art Students' League in New York. She did covers and illustrations for women's and children's magazines. The periodicals she did illustrations for included: *Youth's Companion, Redbook,* and *Sunday Magazine.* Nosworthy was one of the few female illustrators to create her own version of the beautiful American woman. Her portfolio of American beauties was called *A Garden of Girls,* published by R.H. Russell in 1902. Three of the books she illustrated were: Frances Hodgeson Burnett's *The Children's Book* (New York, 1909); Ethel Dow's *The Diary of a Birthday Doll* (Philadelphia, 1908); and William Clark Russell's *Captain Fanny* (New York, 1902). Nosworthy died in Hampton, Conneticut in 1936.
(See cat. no. 102)

THORNTON OAKLEY

Born Pittsburgh, Pennsylvania, 1881. Oakley studied first at the Shady Side Academy and then at the University of Pennsylvania, where he earned a degree in architecture in 1902. Later he studied illustration under Howard Pyle. Oakley's illustrations were published in *National Geographic Magazine, Everybody's, Collier's, Harper's Monthly, Ladies' Home Journal, St. Nicholas Magazine, Outing,* and *Century.* Oakley's best work dealt with scenes of the working class in industrialized America. From 1914 to 1915 he taught at the University of Pennsylvania, and except for 1920, he taught at the Philadelphia Museum's School of Industrial Art from 1914 to 1936. Examples of Oakley's book illustrations are found in Charles King's *To the Front* (New York, 1908); Bradley Gilman's *A Son of the Desert* (New York, 1909); J. Russell Smith's *Story of Iron and Steel* (1913); and Charles Kingsley's *Westward Ho!* (1920). His wife, Amy, wrote several travel books illustrated by Oakley. He died in 1953.
(See cat. no. 103)

WILLIAM OBERHARDT

Born Guttenberg, New Jersey, 1882. Oberhardt was a pupil at the National Academy of Design in New York. He also studied under Carl V. Marr and Ludwig V. Herterich at the Munich Academy of Fine Arts. Oberhardt is remembered as a portrait painter. Many of the famous personalities of his day sat for him, including: Thomas Edison, Dwight Eisenhower, Herbert Hoover, Cardinal Francis J. Spellman, Richard Nixon, and John Foster Dulles. In 1919, the government commissioned Oberhardt to do portraits of the twenty-five members of the Division of Pictorial Publicity. Those portraits are now part of the Archives in Washington, D.C. His book illustration credits included: Edwin Balmer's *The Achievements of Luther Trant* (Boston, 1910); James O. Curwood's *God's Country—and the Women* (New York, 1915); and James Francis Dwyer's *The Green Half-Moon* (Chicago, 1915). Oberhardt also did advertising artwork for the H.J. Heinz Company. He died in Pelham, New York in 1958.
(See cat. no. 104)

ROSE CECIL O'NEILL [LATHAM WILSON]

Born Wilkes-Barre, Pennsylvania, 1874. O'Neill was a self-taught artist, novelist, and poet. In 1893, she moved to New York to attend the Convent of the Sisters of Saint Regis. To pay for her education O'Neill sold illustrations to *Truth, Collier's,* and *Harper's.* Later, her work also appeared in *McClure's Magazine, Woman's Home Companion, Good Housekeeping, Everybody's, Ladies' Home Journal, Life,* and *Puck.* In 1909, she created the "Kewpies" — chubby, adorable babies who won the hearts of the American public. She did advertising work for JELL-O and Edison Phonograph. O'Neill died in Springfield, Missouri in 1944.
(See cat. nos. 105 and 106)

CLARA ELSENE WILLIAMS PECK

Born Allegan, Michigan, 1883. Peck studied at the Minnesota School of Fine Arts, the Philadelphia Academy of the Fine Arts, and under William M. Chase in New York. Many of her illustrations were done for advertisers, notably Proctor and Gamble, Aeolian Company, and Metropolitan Life. Peck illustrated for *St. Nicholas Magazine, Century,* and *Collier's.* She also did book decorations. Some of Peck's book illustrations can be found in Josephine Daskam's *In Border Country* (1909); Sara Hawks Sterling's *A Lady of King Arthur's Court* (Philadelphia, 1907); and *Shakespeare's Sweetheart* (Philadelphia, 1905). Her home was in Palisades Park, New Jersey.
(See cat. nos. 107 and 108)

HENRY JARVIS PECK

Born Galesburg, Illinois, 1880. Peck studied first at the Rhode Island School of Design, and then under Eric Pape in Massachusetts. In 1901, Peck moved to Wilmington, Delaware to study under Howard Pyle. His illustrations sold to most of the leading periodicals, including: *Saturday Evening Post, Harper's, Collier's, Century, Everybody's, Redbook, St. Nicholas Magazine, Scribner's Magazine, Outing, Delineator, Success,* and *Life.* He illustrated Elizabeth Stuart Ward's *The Man in the Case* (New York, 1906) and Frank Lillie Pollock's *The Frozen Fortune* (New York, 1910). Peck travelled in France in 1918. When he returned to the United States, Peck set up studios first in Rhode Island and then in New York.
(See cat. no. 109)

ERNEST CLIFFORD PEIXOTTO

Born San Francisco, California, 1869. Peixotto studied at the San Francisco Art School of Design and in Paris under Benjamin Constant, Lefebvre, and Doucet. He taught at the Art Institute of Chicago from 1907 to 1908. Some of the books he illustrated were: Edith Newbold Wharton's *Italian Backgrounds* (New York, 1905); Mary Noailles Murfree's *The Story of Old Fort London* (New York, 1899); Clayton Meeker Hamilton's *Wanderings* (Garden City, 1925); Theodore Roosevelt's *Life of Cromwell* (1907); and Henry Cabot Lodge's *Story of the Revolution* (New York, 1903). Peixotto travelled widely. He wrote and illustrated his own books: *By Italian Seas* (New York, 1906); *Through the French Provinces* (New York, 1909); *Romantic California* (New York, 1910); *Our Hispanic Southwest* (New York, 1916); *Pacific Shores from Panama* (New York, 1913); and *Through Spain and Portugal* (New York, 1922). Peixotto was one of eight official artists with the American Expeditionary Force sent to Europe in 1918. In 1919, he published *The American Front* (New York, 1919), a narrative and pictorial account of his personal experiences during the war. Peixotto was also a noted muralist. In 1921, the French government appointed him director of the American School of Fine Arts in the Palace of Fontainebleau where he served until 1926. Peixotto died in New York in 1940.
(See cat. no. 110)

GERALD W. PETERS

Peters' illustrations appeared in *Century, Leslie's Illustrated Weekly, Collier's,* and *Scribner's Magazine.* He often picked his subject matter from lives of immigrants and tenement dwellers of New York City. In 1898, he went to Manila, Philippines, where he compiled a travel book called *Picturesque Manila* (1899). In 1913, he illustrated Anna Katherine Green's *The Leavenworth Case.* His home was in Leonia, New Jersey.
(See cat. no. 111)

HERMAN PFEIFER

Born Milwaukee, Wisconsin, 1874. Pfeifer studied at the Royal Academy in Munich, and under Howard Pyle at Chadds Ford, Pennsylvania. His works were published in: *Good Housekeeping, Harper's, Redbook, Saturday Evening Post, McClure's Magazine, Ladies' Home Journal, Circle Magazine,* and *Century.* His book illustration credits included: Lucia Chamberlain's *The Other Side of the Door* (New York, 1909); Frederick S. Isham's *Half a Chance* (Indianapolis, 1909); Jacques Furtrelle's *The Diamond Master* (Indianapolis, 1909); Henry B.M. Watson's *The Castle by the Sea* (Boston, 1909); Frank MacKenzie Savile's *The Pursuit* (Boston, 1910) and *The Road* (Boston, 1911); Sophie Fisher's *The Imprudence of Prue* (Indianapolis, 1911); Jeffery Farnol's *The Amateur Gentleman* (Boston, 1913); Gene Stratton-Porter's *Laddie: A True Blue Story* (New York, 1914); and Grace Louise Smith Richmond's *The Brown Study* (Garden City, 1917). Pfeifer died in 1931.
(See cat. no. 112)

HENRY CLARENCE PITZ

Born Philadelphia, Pennsylvania, 1895. Pitz studied at the Philadelphia College of Art and the Spring Garden Institute. His teachers were Walter Everett and Maurice Bower. Pitz illustrated more than one hundred books during his career. His drawings were also published by *Good Housekeeping, Woman's Home Companion, Country Gentleman, Harper's, Cosmopolitan, Scribner's Magazine, Gourmet, Saturday Evening Post,* and *St. Nicholas Magazine.* His home was in Plymouth Meeting, Pennsylvania. Pitz wrote books and articles about illustrating, among them a biography of Howard Pyle. Pitz died in Delaware in 1976.
(See cat. no. 113)

HARRY SPAFFORD POTTER

Born Detroit, Michigan, 1873. Potter was a pupil of Benjamin Constant, Jean Paul Laurens, and Lucien Simeon in Paris. Potter's illustrations appeared in *Outing, Redbook, Success, St. Nicholas Magazine,* and *Century.* Two books he illustrated included: Harriet Theresa Smith Comstock's *The Place Beyond the Winds* (New York, 1914) and Frank Stockton's *Kate Bonnet* (New York, 1902). Potter died in New York in 1940.
(See cat. no. 114)

JAMES MOORE PRESTON

Born 1873. Preston studied at the Philadelphia Academy of the Fine Arts at the same time as Glackens, Luks, Sloan, and Shinn. He also studied in Paris where he met May Wilson Watkins. They were married in 1903. Preston's illustrations appeared in *Women's Home Companion* and *Success.* The Public Ledger Company published some of his historical drawings in 1922 called *Historic Philadelphia.* He also did commercial illustrating for Calkins and Holden, Inc. and H.J. Heinz Company. Some of Preston's work was exhibited in the Armory Exhibition in New York in 1913. He died in East Hampton, Long Island in 1962.
(See cat. no. 115)

MAY (MARY) WILSON WATKINS PRESTON

Born May Wilson, New York City, 1873. Preston studied at the Art Students' League in New York after her graduation from Oberlin College. She married Thomas Watkins who died two years later. She was a student of James MacNeill Whistler at the World's Art Centre in Paris. In 1903, she met James Preston in Paris and they married. Following her marriage she changed her working signature from May Wilson Watkins to May Wilson Preston. *Harper's Bazar* published her first illustration in 1901. She also worked for: *McClure's Magazine, Scribner's Magazine, Everybody's, Saturday Evening Post, American Magazine, Delineator,* and *Ladies' Home Journal.* She was frequently paired with author Mary Roberts Rinehart, but also illustrated books for: Ring Lardner, F. Scott Fitzgerald, Ellis Parker Butler, Julian Street, Charles Brackett, Wallace Irwin, Joseph Hergesheimer, Sophie Kerr, P.G. Woodhouse, and Alice Duer Miller. Preston died in East Hampton, New York in 1949.
(See cat. nos. 116 and 117)

NORMAN MILLS PRICE

Born Brampton, Ontario, 1877. Price first studied at the Ontario School of Art in Toronto. He and two other art students left the school and worked their way to London, England. After arriving in London, Price studied art at the Goldsmith's Institute and the Westminster School of Art. Later he moved to Paris where he studied under Jean Paul Laurens and Richard Miller at the Académie Julian. Price returned to North America, settled in New York City and began his career as an illustrator. He is noted for the historical accuracy of his illustrations. *Cosmopolitan, American Magazine, Liberty,* and *Woman's Home Companion* published his illustrations, and *St. Nicholas Magazine* frequently used his drawings for cover designs. He was often teamed with authors Frederick Arnold Kummer and Robert W. Chambers. Price illustrated historical books by such authors as: George Sampson, May C. Byron, Dorothea F. Fisher, Flora Warren Seymour, and Rebecca West. Price died in 1951.
(See cat. no. 118)

HENRY PATRICK RALEIGH

Born Portland, Oregon, 1880. Raleigh's family moved to San Francisco when he was eight. As a young man he supported the family working as a clerk in a coffee import business. He also found time to study at the Hopkins Academy in San Francisco. His first art-related job was as a newspaper artist for the *San Francisco Examiner*. While there the owner, William Randolph Hearst, noticed his talent and encouraged him to move to New York. There Raleigh worked for *The World* newspaper and also received illustrating assignments with *Harper's Bazar, Saturday Evening Post, Collier's,* and *Hearst*. He also worked as an advertising artist. After becoming a successful illustrator, he moved to Westport, Connecticut. Edward Ashe, Karl Anderson, Arthur Dove, Guy Pene duBois, Rose O'Neill, George Wright, and Wallace Irving were among his friends and neighbours. Raleigh illustrated: Nalbro Isadorah Bartley's *The Bargain Ture* (Boston, 1918) and *A Woman's Woman* (Boston, 1919); Gelett Burgess' *Mrs. Hope's Husband* (New York, 1917); George Randolph Chester's *Cordelia Blossom* (New York, 1914), *Get-Rich-Quick Wallingford* (Philadelphia, 1908) and *Young Wallingford* (Indianapolis, 1910); William Dean Howell's *The Leatherwood God* (New York, 1916); Arthur Emerson McFarlane's *Behind the Bolted Door* (New York, 1916); Jesse L. Williams' *Remaking Time* (New York, 1916); Henry Rowland's *Pearl Island* (New York, 1919); and Virginia Tracy's *Person Unknown* (New York, 1914). Raleigh died in New York in 1944.
(See cat. no. 119)

CHARLES M. RELYEA

Born Albany, New York, 1863. Relyea studied from 1886 to 1887 under Thomas Eakins at the Pennsylvania Academy of the Fine Arts and later under Frank Vincent DuMond in New York. He illustrated books by such authors as: Ralph Henry Barbour, Amelia E. Barr, Frederick O. Bartlett, Geraldine Bonner, Robert Bowen, James Oliver Curwood, Harris Dickson, Mary Dillon, Mary C. DuBois, Anna Katherine Green, Emilie B. Knipe, Gaston Leroux, Grace Louise Richmond, Jacob August Riis, Thomas Lee Woolwine, O. Henry, Henry Van Dyke, James Whitcomb Riley, and Beatrice Mantle. The leading magazines that purchased his drawings included: *Century, Success,* and *St. Nicholas Magazine*. His home was in New Rochelle, New York. Relyea died in Flushing, New York in 1932.
(See cat. nos. 120, 121, and 122)

T.G. RICHARDSON

Very little is known about Richardson. His career as an illustrator flourished in the 1920s.
(See cat. no. 123)

JACK MANLEY ROSE

Early in his career, Rose sold drawings to *St. Nicholas Magazine*. Books he illustrated included: Jeanette Eaton's *Leader of Destiny: George Washington* (New York, 1938); Grace Rose's travel books *Ports of the Past* (New York, 1941); and *Williamsburg Today and Yesterday* (New York, 1940). Rose also did the murals for an historic house in Annapolis, Maryland.
(See cat. no. 124)

OLIVE RUSH

Born Fairmount, Indiana, 1873. Rush studied art at the Art Students' League in New York under John Twachtman and H. Siddons Mowbray and under Howard Pyle at Wilmington, Delaware. Rush also travelled to Paris to study under Richard Miller. She was trained as a painter and muralist. Later, she returned to the United States, settled in Santa Fe, New Mexico and painted murals. She contributed to *Collier's, Delineator, Good Housekeeping, Ladies' Home Journal, St. Nicholas Magazine, Scribner's Magazine, Sunday Magazine,* and *Woman's Home Companion*. Books illustrated by Rush included: Helen L. Marshall's *A New Mexican Boy* (New York, 1940) and Burton Stevenson's *The Path of Honor* (Philadelphia, 1910). She died in 1966.
(See cat. no. 125)

CHARLES NICOLAS SARKA

Born Chicago, Illinois, 1879. Sarka was an artist with a wanderlust. He travelled to the South Seas, Africa, Tahiti and Morocco. Sarka began his illustration career as a newspaper artist working for papers in Chicago, San Francisco, and New York. He also sold drawings to *Cosmopolitan, Success, American Magazine, Collier's, Everybody's, Leslie's Illustrated Weekly,* and *Judge.* Sarka preferred to work in watercolour and was an active member of the American Watercolor Society. He was also a muralist. In his later years, Sarka spent summers at Canada Lake in New York. He died in 1960. (See cat. no. 126)

OSCAR FREDERICK SCHMIDT

Born 1892. Schmidt studied at the Pratt Institute in Brooklyn and at the Art Students' League in New York. He served in the armed forces during World War One, and after the war he travelled around the world. During his career as an illustrator Schmidt submitted work to *St. Nicholas Magazine, Harper's Monthly, Liberty, Redbook,* and *Saturday Evening Post.* He died in 1957. (See cat. no. 127)

FRANK EARLE SCHOONOVER

Born Oxford, New Jersey, 1877. Schoonover studied at the Drexel Institute in Philadelphia under Howard Pyle and was one of the few students chosen by Pyle to study under him at Chadds Ford, Pennsylvania. He took Pyle's advice to "get involved with one's paintings" seriously. To better understand Indians and Eskimos of Canada, Schoonover made two trips to Hudson Bay to study life in the open. He illustrated more than one hundred novels. Schoonover worked with such authors as: Cummings, Edgar Rice Burroughs, Lucy Foster Madison, James Curwood, William A. Fraser, Rupert S. Holland, and Katherine Grey. Schoonover's work also appeared in most of the major periodicals in the United States. Later in life he taught at the John Herron Art Institute in Indiana. He died in Wilmington, Delaware in 1972. (See cat. nos. 128 and 129)

RAYMOND SISLEY [HERBERT MORTON STOOPS

Born Idaho, 1887. Stoops studied at Utah State College and at the Art Institute of Chicago. By 1910, he was a newspaper artist contributing illustrations to the *San Francisco Call* and the *Chicago Tribune.* During World War One, Stoops served with the 149th Artillery and recorded powerful images of men and war. After the war he settled in New York City and became a noted illustrator of the American beautiful girl. He signed his work either "Raymond Sisley" or "Jeremy Cannon." Stoops died in Mystic, Connecticut in 1948. (See cat. no. 130)

THORNTON DRAKE SKIDMORE

Born Brooklyn, New York, 1884. Skidmore studied naval architecture, but after three years switched to art. He studied under Eric Pape and Howard Pyle. Skidmore's first jobs were as a cartoonist for *The Record, The Globe,* and *The Traveller* — all Boston newspapers. He sold illustrations to *Cosmopolitan, American Magazine, Woman's Home Companion, Everybody's, Ladies' Home Journal, Youth's Companion,* and *Collier's.* He also continued his cartooning career, submitting drawings to *Life.* He illustrated: Samuel White's *Empery* (New York, 1913) and Peter Bernard Kyne's *Cappy Ricks Retires* (New York, 1922). Skidmore died in 1956. (See cat. no. 131)

SARAH KATHERINE SMITH

Born Rio Vista, California, c.1877. Smith studied at the Art Institute of Chicago and under William M. Chase. She attended Wheaton College in Illinois from 1895 to 1898. She later taught there from 1906 to 1908. From 1910 to 1911, Smith attended Howard Pyle's classes at Wilmington, Delaware. Her illustrations appeared in *Outlook, St. Nicholas Magazine,* and *Youth's Companion.* Smith illustrated several books, which included: Clara Murray's *The Wide Awake Fourth Reader* (Boston, 1914); Caroline Frances Burrell's *The Fun of Cooking* (New York, 1915); and Lulu Daniel Hardy's *The Love Cycle* (Boston, 1924). In 1940, she taught at Gulf Park College. (See cat. no. 132)

FRANK SNAPP

Snapp worked for *Judge* and *Collier's*. Examples of his book illustrations are found in the following: Earl Biggers' *Seven Keys of Baldpate* (Indianapolis, 1913); Sewell Ford's *Wilt Thou, Torchy* (New York, 1917); Adele Leuhrmann's *The Curious Case of Marie Dupont* (New York, 1916); Edith Macvane's *Her Word of Honor* (Boston, 1912); Samuel Merwin's *The Trifflers* (Indianapolis, 1916); and Gouverneur Morris' *When My Ship Comes In* (New York, 1919). His home was New York City.
(See cat. no. 133)

PAUL C. STAHR

Born New York City, c.1883. Stahr studied at the National Academy of Design in New York and under John Ward. His periodical illustrations appeared in *Life, Collier's, Harper's Bazar, Judge, American Magazine, Woman's Home Companion,* and *Leslie's Illustrated Weekly*. Books Stahr illustrated included: Ruby Ayres' *A Bachelor Husband* (New York, 1920); Beatrice Baskerville's *The Enchanted Garden* (New York, 1921); Oliver Kent's *Her Heart's Gift* (New York, 1913) and *Her Right Devine* (New York, 1913); Isabel Egenton Ostrander's *Anything Once* (New York, 1920); Perley Poore Sheehand's *If You Believe It, It's So* (New York, 1919); and Nancy M. Woodrow's *The Hornet's Nest* (Boston, 1917). Stahr lived in New York but spent summers in Long Beach, California, where he died in 1953.
(See cat. no. 134)

ALICE BARBER STEPHENS

Born near Salem, New Jersey, 1858. Stephens attended the Philadelphia School of Design for Women. Upon completion she entered the Pennsylvania Academy of the Fine Arts and studied under Thomas Eakins. He was the principal influence on her artistic style. Stephens studied as a wood engraver under Edward Dalziel and worked for a short period as a wood engraver for *Scribner's Magazine*. By 1884, her illustrations were appearing regularly in the leading periodicals. In 1886, Stephens studied at the Académie Julian and Académie Colarossi in Paris. She illustrated *Little Women* (1902) and *Under the Lilacs* (1905) by Louisa May Alcott. Her work was well respected and authors James Lane Allen and Arthur Conan Doyle specifically requested that she illustrate their books. Stephens also did illustrations for:

Margaret Deland, Mary Freeman, Hamlin Garland, Harriet Spofford, Frank Stockton, and Kate Douglas Wiggin. Periodicals which published her illustrations included: *McClure's, Scribner's Magazine, Harper's, Century, Ladies' Home Journal,* and *St. Nicholas Magazine*. Stephens also worked for Proctor & Gamble as an advertising artist. Her home was in Moyland, Pennsylvania where she died in 1932.
(See cat. nos. 135 and 136)

WALTER KING STONE

Born New York state, 1875. Stone studied at the Rochester Mechanics' Institute and at the Pratt Institute in Brooklyn, New York. His illustrations, chiefly of animals, appeared in *Scribner's Magazine, Century,* and *Harper's*. Stone was often teamed with authors Walter Prichard Eaton and Grace Seton. In 1920, Stone began a teaching career in the fine arts at Cornell University in Ithaca, New York, a position he held for twenty-two years. He was a popular professor and friends affectionately called him "Stony." He died in Ithaca in 1949.
(See cat. no. 137)

THURE de THULSTRUP

Born Stockholm, Sweden, 1848. Thulstrup fought in the Franco-Prussian War and then immigrated to the United States in 1873. He studied at the Art Students' League in New York and worked as a staff artist for *Frank Leslie's Illustrated Magazine* and the *New York Daily Graphic*. During the Spanish-American War, Thulstrup was an artist-correspondent for *Harper's Weekly* and *Collier's*. His work frequently appeared in the pages of *Century, Scribner's Magazine, Ladies' Home Journal, Cosmopolitan,* and other leading periodicals. Authors for whom he illustrated included: Kirk Munroe, Arthur Conan Doyle, George Croley, Henry Blake Fuller, and Francis Hopkinson Smith. Thulstrup died in New York in 1930.
(See cat. no. 138)

MAUD THURSTON

Little is known about Maud Thurston. She worked for *Ladies' Home Journal* and *Life*.
(See cat. no. 139)

OTTO TOASPERN

Born Brooklyn, New York, 1863. Toaspern studied at the Royal Academy of Fine Arts in Munich. He was a cartoonist with *Life*, and was recognized for his caricatures of famous personalities. Toaspern's work also appeared in *Puck* and *Redbook*. He illustrated *The Balance of Power* by Arthur Goodrich (New York, 1907). Toaspern died in 1940.
(See cat. no. 140)

GEORGE TIMOTHY TOBIN

Born Weybridge, Vermont, 1864. Tobin studied under George de Forest-Brush at the Art Students' League in New York. His drawings were published by *Century, Scribner's Magazine, The Lamp,* and *St. Nicholas Magazine.* Books he illustrated included: Guy Fitch Phelps' *The Mountains of the Morning* (New York, 1916); Charles Dickens' *A Christmas Carol* (New York, 1899); and Rudyard Kipling's *Recessional* (New York, 1898). Tobin was also a noted portrait painter. Among his subjects were: Woodrow Wilson, Theodore Roosevelt, Charles Evans Hughes, Charles W. Eliot, Charles Dana Gibson, Lady Randolph Churchill, and Pope Pius X. During his career, Tobin made his home in New Rochelle, New York, but retired to St. Albans, Vermont, where he died in 1956.
(See cat. no. 141)

STUART TRAVIS

Born 1868. Travis was both an illustrator and muralist. He worked for *Saturday Evening Post*. Books he illustrated included: William MacLeod's *A Daughter of Raasay* (New York, 1902) and Augusta Jane Wilson's *Devota* (New York, 1907). Travis was a consulting artist at the Addison Gallery of American Art at Phillips Academy in Andover, Massachusetts. He died in 1942.
(See cat. no. 142)

LESLIE HOLLAND TURNER

Born Cisco, Texas, 1900. Turner studied at Southern Methodist University from 1918 to 1922. He left school to do freelance artwork in Dallas, then moved to Colorado for a period, and finally to New York in 1933. He achieved great popularity with the comic strip "Captain Easy." Turner also sold drawings to *Judge, Saturday Evening Post, Scribner's Magazine, Ladies' Home Journal, St. Nicholas Magazine,* and *Pictorial Review.* An example of Turner's book illustration is found in Henry Augustus Shute's *Plupy, Beany and Pewt* (Philadelphia, 1926).
(See cat. no. 143)

CHARLOTTE WEBER-DITZLER

Born Philadelphia, Pennsylvania, 1877. Weber-Ditzler studied art under Schmidt and Fehr in Munich and under Howard Pyle at Chadds Ford, Pennsylvania. Her illustrations appeared in *Sunday Magazine, Redbook, Saturday Evening Post,* and *Success.* Weber-Ditzler illustrated such books as: Jeffery Farnol's *My Lady Caprice* (New York, 1907); Anne French's *When a Woman Proposes* (Boston, 1911); Joseph C. Lincoln's *Cap'n Eri* (New York, 1904); William Orcutt's *The Flower of Destiny* (Chicago, 1905); Charles Felton Pidgin's *The Letter H* (New York, 1904); Margaret Potter's *The Castle of Twilight* (Chicago, 1903); Henry Cottrell Rowland's *The Windward, The Story of a Stormy Course* (New York, 1904); and L.N. Way's *The Call of the Heart* (New York, 1909). Weber-Ditzler died in 1958.
(See cat. no. 144)

IRVING RAMSAY WILES

Born Utica, New York, 1861. Wiles studied at the Art Students' League in New York, and then for two years in Paris under Lefebvre and Carolus-Duran. He was also influenced by his artist-father L.M. Wiles, William M. Chase, and J.C. Beckwith. His drawings were published by *Ladies' Home Companion, Century, Harper's, Scribner's Magazine,* and *St. Nicholas Magazine.* Wiles illustrated such books as: Henry Cuyler Bunner's *Jersey Street and Jersey Land* (New York, 1896); Edward Eggleston's *Stories of American Life and Adventure* (New York, 1905); Robert Grant's *The Bachelor's Christmas* (New York, 1895); and Constance Harrison's *A Bachelor Maid* (New York, 1894). Wiles was also a painter and muralist. He lived in New York, although he spent summers in Peconic, Long Island. He died in 1948.
(See cat. no. 145)

ADA CLENDENIN WILLIAMSON

Born Camden, New Jersey, 1880. Williamson grew up in West Chester, Pennsylvania. She moved to Philadelphia in 1896. She studied at the Drexel Institute in Philadelphia from 1896 to 1908, and then under Howard Pyle. Williamson also studied at the Pennsylvania Academy of the Fine Arts under William M. Chase and Cecilia Beaux. Williamson's magazine illustrations appeared in *Harper's*, *St. Nicholas Magazine*, *Delineator*, *Woman's Home Companion*, *Youth's Companion*, and *House and Garden*. Her book illustrations can be found in the following: Inez Irwin's *Janey* (New York, 1911); Rebecca Newman Porter's *The Girl from Four Corners* (New York, 1920); Perley Poore Sheehan's *If You Believe It, It's So* (New York, 1919); and Katherine Taylor's *Real Stuff* (New York, 1921). Williamson died in Ogunquit, Maine in 1958.
(See cat. no. 146)

ALICE BEACH WINTER

Born Greenridge, Missouri, 1877. Winter studied at the St. Louis School of Fine Arts and the Art Students' League in New York. Influential teachers included: John Fry, Charles Von Saltza, John Twachtman, and George de Forest-Brush. Winter specialized in drawings of children. Her periodical illustrations were published in *Sunday Magazine* and *Delineator*. She also designed many advertisements for the Proctor & Gamble Company. Her husband was artist and illustrator, Charles Allan Winter. Winter lived in St. Louis, Missouri; East Pasadena, California; and in East Gloucester, Massachusetts. She died in 1970.
(See cat. no. 147)

FRANKLIN T. WOOD

Born Hyde Park, Massachusetts, 1887. Wood studied at the Art Students' League in New York, and in Europe. His periodical illustrations were published in *Youth's Companion*. He illustrated George Buffum's *Smith of Bearlity* (New York, 1906). Wood is also remembered as an etcher, wood carver, and ship model builder. He died in Rutland, Massachusetts in 1945.
(See cat. no. 148)

GEORGE HAND WRIGHT

Born Fox Chase, Pennsylvania, 1872. Wright went to New York where he worked as a jewellery designer. He studied at the Spring Garden Institute in Philadelphia and the Pennsylvania Academy of the Fine Arts. His work appeared in *Scribner's Magazine*, *Collier's*, *Harper's*, *Century*, and *Saturday Evening Post*. He illustrated many books, among them: Thomas Nelson Page's *Gordon Keith* (New York, 1903); Francis Hopkinson Smith's *Felix O'Day* (New York, 1915); and Grace Alexander's *Judith* (New York, 1906). Other illustrations by Wright can be found in the books of Henry Curran, Thomas Dixon, Louis Dodge, Emerson Hough, Henry B. Needham, Grant Showerman, and Kate Douglas Wiggin. Wright died in Westport, Connecticut in 1951.
(See cat. nos. 149, 150, and 151)

FREDERICK COFFAY YOHN

Born Indianapolis, Indiana, 1875. Yohn studied at the Indianapolis Art School and the Art Students' League in New York. His most influential teacher was H. Siddons Mowbray. Yohn published his first illustration with *Harper's*. This opened the way for publications in *Scribner's Magazine*, *Collier's*, *Harper's Round Table*, and other leading periocials. He illustrated such books as: Molly Seawell's *Virginia Cavalier* (New York, 1896); Francis Hopkinson Smith's *Colonel Carter's Christmas* (New York, 1903); and Kate Douglas Wiggin's *New Chronicles of Rebecca* (1907). Yohn died in Norwalk, Connecticut in 1933.
(See cat. no. 152)

ARTIST'S BIOGRAPHIES WERE COMPILED FROM THE FOLLOWING:

REFERENCES:

Biographical Sketches of American Artists. Lansing, Michigan: Mich. State Library, 1924.

Dictionnaire critique et documentaire des Peintres, Sculpteurs, Dessinateurs et Graveurs. E. Benezit, Libraire Grund, 1950.

Dictionary of American Biography; Under the Auspices of the American Council of Learned Societies. Allen Johnson and Dumas Malone, ed. New York: Charles Scribner's Sons, 1964.

Dictionary of Women Artists: An International Dictionary of Women Artists Born Before 1900. Chris Petteys with Hazel Gustow, Ferris Olin and Verna Ritchie. Boston: G.K. Hall & Co., 1985.

Illustrators of Children's Books. Bertha E. Mahony, Louise Payson Latimer, and Beulah Folmsbee, comp. Boston: The Horn Book, 1947.

The Illustrators in America, 1900-1960. Walter Reed, ed., New York: Reinhold Publishing Corporation, 1963.

The Illustrator in America, 1880-1980: A Century of Illustration. Walt and Roger Reed, eds., New York: Madison Square Press, in association with The Society of Illustrators, 1984.

Who Was Who in American Art: Compiled from the original thirty-four volumes of American Art Annual and Who's Who in Art, biographies of American artists active from 1898-1947. Peter Hastings Falk, ed. Madison, Conn.: Sound View Press, 1985.

200 Years of American Illustration. Henry Pitz, New York: Random House, in association with The Society of Illustrators, 1977.

New York Times, obituaries.

EXHIBITION CATALOGUES:

Delaware Art Museum. *The Golden Age of American Illustration, 1880-1914.* Wilmington: The Wilmington Society of the Fine Arts, 1972.

Delaware Art Museum. *A Small School of Art: The Students of Howard Pyle.* Rowland Elzea and Elizabeth H. Hawkes, eds., Wilmington: Delaware Art Museum, 1972.

Grunwald Center for the Graphic Arts. *The American Personality - The Artist-Illustrator of Life in the United States, 1860-1930.* Los Angeles: University of California, Los Angeles, 1976.

The Brooklyn Museum. *A Century of American Illustration.* Brooklyn: The Brooklyn Museum, 1972.

ARCHIVES:

Clipping files on artists at the Free Library of Philadelphia, the Library of Congress, the Boston Public Library, the Delaware Museum of Art, The Brandywine River Museum, and the New York Public Library.

BIBLIOGRAPHY

Abbott, Charles D. *Howard Pyle, a Chronicle.*
New York: Harper & Brothers, 1935.

Allen, Douglas and Allen, Douglas Jr. *N.C. Wyeth:
the Collected Paintings, Illustrations and Murals.*
New York: Crown, 1972.

Armstrong, Regina. "New Leaders in American
Illustration." Parts 1-5. *The Bookman* 10 (February
1900): 548-55; 11 (March, April, May, June 1900):
49-55, 140-48; 244-52, 334-41.

_____. "Representative American Woman
Illustrators: The Child Interpreters." Parts 1-4. *The
Critic* 36 (May, June 1900): 417-23; 520-29; 37
(July, August 1900): 43-54; 131-41.

Bolton, Theodore. *American Book Illustrators:
Bibliographic Check Lists of 123 Artists.* New York:
R.R. Bowker Co., 1938.

"Book and Magazine Illustration." *The Bookman* 17
(August 1903): 651-3.

Bradley, Will. "The Art of Illustration." *The Nation* 97
(July 1913): 42-3.

Book of Notable American Illustrators. New York:
The Walter Engraving Co., 1926, 1927.

The Brandywine River Museum. *Alice Barber Stephens:
A Pioneer Woman Illustrator.* Essay by Ann
Barton Brown. Chadds Ford, Pa.: Brandywine
River Museum, 1984.

_____. *The Art of American Illustration.* Essay by
Joan H. Gorman. Chadds Ford, Pa.: The
Brandywine River Museum, 1976.

_____. *The Brandywine Heritage.* Foreword by
Richard McLanathan. Chadds Ford, Pa.: The
Brandywine River Museum, 1971.

_____. *Charlotte Harding: An Illustrator in
Philadelphia.* Essay by Ann Barton Brown. Chadds
Ford, Pa.: The Brandywine River Museum, 1982.

_____. *Thornton Oakley.* Essay by Gene E. Harris.
Chadds Ford, Pa.: The Brandywine River Museum,
1983.

_____. *Women Artists in the Howard Pyle
Tradition.* Introduction by Anne E. Mayer. Chadds
Ford, Pa.: The Brandywine River Museum, 1975.

The Brooklyn Museum, New York. *A Century of
American Illustration.* Introduction by Duncan F.
Cameron; essays by Linda S. Ferber and Robin E.
Brown. New York: The Brooklyn Museum Press,
1972.

Burnham, Laurence. "The Modern Hero in Illustration."
The Bookman (July 1907): 502-10.

_____. "The Modern Heroine in Illustration."
The Bookman (1907): 191-99.

Caffin, Charles H. "A Note on American Illustration."
Independent 63 (November 1907): 1217-19.

Coffin, William A. "American Illustration of To-Day."
Scribner's Monthly 11 (January 1892): 106-17; 11
(February 1892): 117-205; 11 (March 1892): 333-49.

Delaware Art Museum. *The American Magazine,
1890-1940.* Essays by Rowland Elzea, Dorey
Schmidt, Margaret Cohen, Michael Barson, Peter
Rollins, Elizabeth Hawkes, Martha Cooper, George
Straley, and Felice Jo Lamden. Wilmington, Del.:
Delaware Art Museum, 1979.

_____. *City Life Illustrated, 1890-1940.* Wilmington,
Del.: Delaware Art Museum, 1980.

_____. *The Golden Age of American Illustration,
1880-1914.* Introduction by Rowland Elzea.
Wilmington, Del.: Wilmington Society of the Fine
Arts, 1972.

_____. *A Small School of Art: The Students of
Howard Pyle.* Rowland Elzea and Betsey Hawkes,
ed. Wilmington, Del.: Delaware Art Museum, 1980.

Dodd, Loring Holmes. *A Generation of Illustrators and
Etchers.* Boston: Chapman & Grimes, 1960.

Eastman, Max. *Journalism Versus Art.* New York:
Knopf, n.d.

Edwards, George Wharton. "The Illustration of Books."
The Outlook 57 (December 4, 1897): 816-24.

Ewers, John. *Artists of the Old West.* New York:
Doubleday & Co., 1973.

Federal Schools. *Modern Illustrating.* 1931.

"Foremost American Illustrators." *Craftsman* 17 (1909):
266-80.

Fowler, Grace Alexander. "Among the Illustrators." *Harper's Bazar* 39 (1905): 528-34.

Gallatin, Albert Eugene. *Art and The Great War.* New York: E.P. Dutton & Co., 1919.

Getchell, Margaret C. "In and Out of Germany with a Philadelphia Artist." *Public Ledger (Philadelphia) Magazine.* March 16, 1919.

Glenbow Museum. *Charles Livingston Bull.* Essay by Peter White. Calgary, Alberta: Glenbow-Alberta Institute, 1979.

Grunwald Center for the Graphic Arts. *The American Personality: The Artist-Illustrator of Life in the United States, 1860-1930.* Introduction by E. Maurice Bloch. Essays by Teona Tone Gneiting, Cheryl Jones, Judy L. Larson, Francis Martin, Jr., Phyllis Peet, Irene Sawyer, Wahneta T. Robinson, Gina Strumwasser, Nancy Thomas and Joseph Young. Los Angeles: University of California, Los Angeles, 1976.

Guptill, Arthur L. *Norman Rockwell, Illustrator.* New York: Watson-Guptill, 1975.

Harding, George. "The American Artist at the Front." *The American Magazine of Art* 10 (October 1919): 451-456.

Hoeber, Arthur. "A Century of American Illustration." Parts 1-3. *The Bookman* 8 (December 1898, January, February 1899): 317-24, 429-39, 540-48.

Houghton Library, Harvard University. *Drawings for Book Illustration - The Hofer Collection.* Essay by David P. Becker. Cambridge, Mass.: Harvard University, Department of Printing and Graphic Arts, 1980.

Hydeman, Sidney. *How to Illustrate for Money.* New York: Harper & Bros., 1936.

Illustrators of Children's Books. Bertha E. Mahony, Louise Payson Latimer, and Beulah Folmsbee, compls. Boston: The Horn Book, 1947.

Jenks, Tudor. "The Decadence of Illustration." *Independent* 51 (December 1899): 3487-89.

Jussim, Estelle. *Visual Communication and the Graphic Arts.* New York and London: R.R. Bowker Co., 1974.

Ludwig, Coy. *Maxfield Parrish.* New York: Watson-Guptill, 1973.

"Magazine Art in America as Diagnosed by an Impatient Editor." *Current Opinion* 58 (February 1915): 117.

Memphis Brooks Museum of Art. *Howard Pyle and the Wyeths: Four Generations of American Imagination.* Essays by Howard P. Brokaw and Douglas K.S. Hyland. Memphis: Memphis Brooks Museum of Art, 1983.

Meyer, Susan E. *America's Great Illustrators.* New York: Galahad Books, 1978.

The Montclair Art Museum. *Charles Parsons and his Domain: An Exhibition of 19th Century American Illustration.* Montclair, N.J.: Montclair Art Museum, 1958.

Mott, Frank Luther. *American Journalism.* New York: Macmillian Co., 1950.

_____. *A History of American Magazines.* vol. 1: New York: D. Appleton & Co., 1930; vol. 2-5: Cambridge, Mass.: Harvard University Press, 1938-1968.

Museum of Fine Arts. *The Artist and the Book In Western Europe and the United States (1860-1960).* Introduction by Philip Hofer. Cambridge, Mass: Harvard College Library, Department of Printing and Graphic Arts, 1961.

The New Britain Museum of American Art. *The Sanford Low Memorial Collection of American Illustration.* New Britain, Conn.: The New Britain Museum of American Art, 1972.

North, Elizabeth D. "Women Illustrators of Child Life." *The Outlook* 78 (October 1904): 270-80.

Pennell, Joseph. *The Adventures of an Illustrator.* London: T. Fisher Unwin Ltd., 1925.

_____. *Modern Illustration.* London and New York: G. Bell & Sons, 1895.

Perlman, Bennard B. *The Golden Age of American Illustration: F.R. Gruger and his Circle.* Westport, Conn.: North Light Publishers, 1978.

Pitz, Henry Clarence. *The Brandywine Tradition.* Boston: Houghton-Mifflin Co., 1969.

_____. *Howard Pyle: Writer, Illustrator, Founder of the Brandywine Tradition.* New York: Clarkson Potter, 1975.

_____. *The Practice of Illustration.* New York: Watson-Guptill, 1947.

_____. *A Treasury of American Book Illustration.* New York: Watson-Guptill, 1947.

_____. *200 Years of American Illustration.* New York: Random House, in association with The Society of Illustrators, 1977.

Reed, Walt, ed. *The Illustrator in America, 1900-1960s.* New York: Reinhold Publishing Co., 1966.

Santa Barbara Museum of Art. *Enchanted Images: American Children's Illustration 1850-1925.* Essay by Judy L. Larson. Santa Barbara, Ca.: Santa Barbara Museum of Art, 1980.

Schnessel, S. Michael. *Jessie Willcox Smith.* New York: Thomas Y. Crowell, 1977.

Smith, Francis Hopkinson. *American Illustrators.* New York: Charles Scribner's Sons, 1892.

Stote, Amos. "The Illustrator and his Income." *The Bookman* 28 (September 1908): 21-26.

Street, Julian. "In Justice to the Illustrator." *The Bookman* 58 (September 1923): 1-4.

Taft, Robert. *Artists and Illustrators of the Old West.* New York: Charles Scribner's Sons, 1953.

Tebbel, John. *A History of Book Publishing in the United States.* Vol. 2. New York: R.R. Bowker, 1975.

Thwaite, Mary F. *From Primer to Pleasure in Reading.* London: Library Association, 1972.

Watson, Ernest W. *Forty Illustrators and How They Work.* New York: Watson-Guptill, 1946.

Weitenkampf, Frank. *American Graphic Art.* New York: Johnson Reprint Corp., 1970.

_____. *The Illustrated Book.* Cambridge, Mass.: Harvard University Press, 1938.

_____. "The Illustrator's Job." *The Bookman* 60 (September 1924): 182-85.

_____. "Trend in American Book Illustration." *International Studio* 82 (December 1925): 199-202.

Willsie, Honore. "Charles Dana Gibson Mobilizes American Illustrators." *Delineator* 93 (November 1918): 16.

Wyeth, N.C. "For Better Illustration." *Scribner's Magazine* 66 (1919): 638-42.

CATALOGUE OF THE EXHIBITION

All dimensions denote sheet size unless otherwise indicated, and in all cases height precedes width measurement.

The titles for illustrations in this exhibition have been taken from the published titles. When such a title is not available, the title inscribed by the artist on the work has been used. In cases where neither a published title nor an artist's inscription is available, a cataloguer's descriptive title, enclosed within square brackets, has been used.

* Denotes work illustrated in colour.

KARL ANDERSON

1. "Children of Eden," October, 1905
gouache, watercolour and graphite
52.5 x 51.5 cm
R624.3007

2. [Couple by the train]
gouache, watercolour and graphite
39.0 x 34.2 cm
R624.2890
Illustrated page 81

EDMUND MARION ASHE

3. "He stands with his back to the door, a barker in each fist."
for: "The Man in Black" by H.B. Marriott Watson in *Collier's Weekly*, January, 1904
gouache and graphite
54.5 x 44.3 cm
R624.3268

WILLIAM JAMES AYLWARD

4. "Jump! Jump for your life!"
for: "The Last Battle Ship" by Morgan Robertson in *Success Magazine*, June, 1908
gouache, watercolour and graphite
49.0 x 39.9 cm
R624.1349

* 5. "St. Lawrence River"
for: *Collier's*
oil on canvas
61.2 x 91.5 cm
R392.1
Illustrated page 51

GEORGE WATSON BARRATT

6. "Forty miles from anywhere and the parson away on vacation"
for: *Life*, vol. 53, 1909
charcoal, watercolour and graphite
70.4 x 52.8 cm (image)
70.8 x 53.6 cm (sheet)
R624.2134

EDWIN F. BAYHA

7. "Mr. Blanchard didn't stop for argument, but ran across the bridge."
for: "Men Who Do Things" by Russell Bond in *St. Nicholas Magazine*, June, 1913
charcoal
58.1 x 42.7 cm
R624.2339

ARTHUR ERNEST BECHER

8. " 'Ah! Mat Corbin!' she said as he came up the steps. 'We've been waitin' for you, us two ladies...Where is Molly Rafferty? Do you know?' "
for: "Molly Rafferty" by Evelyn Gill Klahr in *Collier's*, September, 1914
graphite
40.6 x 53.3 cm
R624.2512

9. "Ye-e-e-e-ow! Take another, Tommy! Slide! Sli-i-i-i-de! All right, I'll get 'em together after the game. Ain't this some game?"
for: "The Game and the Strike" by Edward Speya in *Collier's*, 1913
graphite and gouache
43.1 x 56.6 cm
R624.1255
Illustrated page 111

WLADYSLAW THEODOR BENDA

10. [Woman reading letter]
unpublished drawing submitted to *Associated Sunday Magazine*, 1905
charcoal
72.2 x 44.2 cm
R624.2348

GERRIT ALBERTUS BÉNEKER

11. "While the cheers of the Benevolent Picklers rent the air"
for: "The Casey-Murphy Handicap" by Ellis Parker Butler in *Success Magazine*, August, 1906
charcoal and watercolour
38.0 x 50.8 cm
R624.3244

MARJORIE TORRE and T.M. BEVANS

12. "The little lady of the Manor 'Blesses' the Grand old Apple Orchard"
for: "The Little Queen of Twelfth Night" in *St. Nicholas Magazine*, January, 1915
graphite and ink
21.7 x 35.5 cm (image)
24.0 x 38.1 cm (sheet)
R624.3421
Illustrated page 102

BINNER ENGRAVING COMPANY OF CHICAGO - anonymous artist

13. "A medium of Strength"
Cover for: *Success*
gouache, watercolour, ink and graphite
43.8 x 34.8 cm
R624.2919

HANSON BOOTH

14. [Saying goodbye to a man on a horse]
charcoal
49.4 x 60.1 cm
R624.1218

15. "The Mischief Maker"
charcoal
53.4 x 38.1 cm (image)
55.9 x 40.5 cm (sheet)
R624.4164

ARMAND BOTH

16. [Couple discovered in the Garden]
charcoal
61.9 x 44.2 cm
R624.1220

17. "Thou dost well to entrust thy business to Ping"
for: "The Prideau Murder" by David Gray in *Collier's*, March, 1912
charcoal and watercolour
48.0 x 35.0 cm
R624.2914

MAURICE L. BOWER

18. "The door swung back, and a knight stood there"
for: "The Adventure of the High King" by Clara Platt Meadowcraft in *St. Nicholas Magazine*, December, 1919
charcoal and ink
69.9 x 45.0 cm
R624.1254
Illustrated page 86

19. "The Adventure of the Knight of the Singing Sword"
Endpiece for: "The Adventure of the Knight of the Singing Sword"
by Clara Platt Meadowcraft in
St. Nicholas Magazine, August, 1919
charcoal and ink
36.0 x 53.0 cm
R624.4401
Illustrated page 99

M. LEONE BRACKER

20. "What?...It's gone, man, the skull is gone!!"
Frontispiece for: *Wandering Ghosts*,
by Francis Marion Crawford
Macmillan Company, New York, 1911
charcoal and gouache
61.1 x 39.2 cm.
R624.1259
Illustrated page 93

21. [Woman struggling out of man's arms]
charcoal
61.1 x 39.2 cm.
R624.1379

PAUL BRANSOM

22. "Mary thrust her long-muzzled head around from behind her partners, and wagged her ears and stared"
for: "Brannigan's Mary" by Charles G.D. Roberts in *Cosmopolitan*, May, 1914
charcoal and gouache
44.5 x 30.5 cm.
R624.2628

23. "Ef we don't make Conroy's camp purty soon, we'll hav to — well, it'll be up to Mary."
for: "Brannigan's Mary" by Charles G.D. Roberts in *Cosmopolitan*, May, 1914
charcoal, gouache and ink
45.2 x 31.3 cm.
R624.2609
Illustrated page 97

GEORGE BREHM

24. "He was...looking out to sea"
for: "Break O' Day" by Justus Miles Forman
in *Collier's*, March, 1908
charcoal, watercolour and crayon
61.4 x 46.3 cm.
R624.4

WORTH BREHM

25. "What did you do with that cream? Don't try to lie out of it, sir! You have hidden it to spite me. Answer this instant!"
for: "Digging Out A Nobleman"
by Ceylon Hollingsworth
in *Collier's*, March 20, 1915
charcoal
46.3 x 43.0 cm.
R624.1112

ARTHUR WILLIAM BROWN

26. "I do n't think, looking it over, I did the wrong thing; I could n't tell how she might turn out"
for: "Beneficiary" by Thomas Beer
in *Century Illustrated Magazine*, August, 1918
watercolour and graphite
29.4 x 40.2 cm
R624.1861
Illustrated page 48

27. "For a moment neither moved nor spoke"
for: "You Just Can't Wait" by Oscar Graeve
in *Collier's*, June, 1918
crayon and watercolour
32.6 x 28.8 cm
R624.648

28. "The first thing I did was to sell the landlady some pictures for a meal ticket"
for: "Hard Luck" by Charles N. Crewdson
in *Success Magazine*, November, 1909
watercolour and crayon
25.5 x 20.4 cm
R264.3428

LEIGHTON BUDD

29. "Beef a la Mode"
Cover design for: *Puck*, July, 1910
watercolour and gouache over printed lithograph
35.9 x 27.6 cm
R624.2248

CHARLES LIVINGSTON BULL

* **30.** "Nothing is to be heard except the low swish of branches"
for: "The Jungle Drama" by C. William Beebe
in *Success Magazine*, June, 1907
gouache, watercolour, ink and charcoal
27.6 x 18.8 cm
66.31.20
Illustrated page 53

* **31.** [Fox chasing cardinal]
watercolour, gouache, charcoal and ink
46.0 x 35.6 cm
66.31.9
Illustrated page 57

JOHN HARMON CASSEL

32. "The engineer had jumped down beside her, and she was explaining to him what the trouble was."
for: "In the Toils of Fate"
by Virginia Mitchell Wheat in
St. Nicholas Magazine, 1907
oil on canvas
50.3 x 75.6 cm (image)
54.7 x 79.9 cm (sheet)
R624.3684

J. ANDRÉ CASTAIGNE

33. [Horseback riders] 1893
charcoal, ink and watercolour
28.7 x 35.7 cm
R624.2130

WILL COLBY

34. "It do be terrible the price some men ask to pay to learn a bitter lesson"
for: "The Home-coming of Katie Devlin"
by William Mailly in *Success Magazine*, 1910
watercolour and ink
31.1 x 41.9 cm
R624.1314

SEWELL COLLINS

35. "I flatter myself that this farce will be one of the best things of the season" —
"Yes, but it's not to be laughed at."
for: *Life*, May, 1903
crayon and gouache
38.0 x 47.5 cm.
R624.1599

FANNY YOUNG CORY

36. [Woman with a candle]
St. Nicholas Magazine
ink and graphite
37.0 x 24.5 cm
R624.1886

PERCY ELTON COWEN

37. " 'There is none aboard the Sunda shall command her now!' he cried with his great voice."
for: "The Blood of Admirals"
by Percy Adams Hutchinson
in *Collier's*, April, 1915
charcoal and watercolour
43.5 x 42.3 cm
R624.1312
Illustrated page 85

PALMER COX

38. [Brownies in the Arctic Ocean]
for: "The Brownies around the World"
ink
21.3 x 7.4 cm
R392.61.5

39. [Brownies and the Ostrich]
for: "The Brownies around the World"
ink
27.9 x 21.9 cm
R392.62.1

40. [Brownies under a Haystack]
for: "Haymaking"
ink
20.0 x 18.5 cm
R392.58.5a

41. [Brownies in a Hay Wagon]
for: "Haymaking"
ink and gouache
14.7 x 16.6 cm
R392.58.2
Illustrated page 101

42. [Brownies on Deck]
for: "The Brownies on the Steamship"
ink
8.0 x 19.5 cm
R392.60.8a

43. [Brownies on Deck]
for: "The Brownies on the Steamship"
ink
8.7 x 18.9 cm
R392.60.8b

WILL CRAWFORD

44. "The Deserter"
[heading] for: "The Deserter" by Berton Braley
in *Puck*, May, 1913
ink
43.8 x 29.8 cm
R624.81
Illustrated page 44

MARGUERITE LOFFT DE ANGELI

45. "Louise loved every inch of
the Royal Park"
for: "Sunny Vigee"
by Katherine Dunlap Cather
in *St. Nicholas Magazine*, January, 1924
charcoal
32.7 x 65.8 cm
R624.2136

CLYDE OSMER DE LAND

46. "There was a Meeting of the Stad Huis
Square, led by Dirck Philipse, the Carpenter"
for: "The Story of Barnaby Lee"
by John Bennett in *St. Nicholas Magazine*, 1902
charcoal, gouache, and ink
61.0 x 44.4 cm
R624.1826

HAROLD S. DE LAY

47. " 'How long have you been here?'
asked Tommy."
for: "Lucky Joe" by Henry Gardner Hunting
in *St. Nicholas Magazine*, October, 1907
crayon, watercolour, gouache and graphite
40.7 x 40.7 cm
R624.3702

WALTER DE MARIS

48. "Bridget, this kitchen smells atrocious. If
you must have that policeman call on you, tell
him not to smoke that vile tobacco." "Sure, an'
Tim says the same. He does be wonderin' how
a gentleman like yourself can smoke sich stuff."
for: *Puck*, October, 1916
charcoal, gouache and ink
47.2 x 56.5 cm
R624.3704

WILLIAM WALLACE DENSLOW

49. "The Health Brigade"
for: a post card design for children [?], 1913
gouache, watercolour and ink
38.4 x 28.3 cm
R624.3240

ARTHUR GARFIELD DOVE

50. "J. Harvey Smith had gazed upon the
group for an instant, had turned pale,
and then - pandemonium!"
for: "Helmstaedter's Piano Home"
by William Hamilton Osborne
in *Success Magazine*, August, 1907
ink, charcoal, watercolour, gouache and crayon
32.0 x 47.2 cm
R624.1880
Illustrated page 36

GEORGE WHARTON EDWARDS

51. "A Dutch Kitchen" c.1908
gouache and watercolour
45.5 x 60.0 cm
R624.2632
Illustrated page 24

ROBERT EDWARDS

52. [Man and woman at desk]
charcoal and watercolour
58.4 x 49.6 cm
R624.3879

WALTER HUNT EVERETT

53. "Monks removing their treasures to a
secret hiding place"
for: "Some Buried Treasure" by Broughton
Brandenburg in *Associated Sunday Magazine*,
December, 1906
charcoal, gouache and ink
28.0 x 45.7 cm
R624.3614

DENMAN FINK

54. "To me he was great, a stranger, as some
infant who born centuries ago to a wild and
nomad woman in Tartary, lived but an hour..."
for: "Benito Perino Migrator"
by Richard Washburn Child
in *Collier's*, March, 1908
watercolour
55.2 x 37.7 cm.
R624.1164
Illustrated page 121

BLANCHE V. FISHER [GREER]

55. [Girl crying over broken doll]
Century Illustrated Magazine, 1907
ink, watercolour and graphite
20.4 x 22.5 cm
R624.3401

56. "I want to be a pirate / And sail upon the
sea / And wear a sword so no one dare / Say
'do' and 'don't' to me / ..."
for: "The Pirate" by H. Sharpsteen in
St. Nicholas Magazine, June, 1906
charcoal, watercolour, varnish and ink
53.5 x 38.4 cm
R624.1427
Illustrated page 47

HARRISON FISHER

57. "A Definition.
Miss Askin. — 'What is a plunger, Mr. Ticker?'
Mr. Ticker. — 'A Plunger is a man who, sooner
or later, takes a dive and does n't come up!'"
[cartoon] for: *Puck*, June, 1899
crayon, gouache and graphite
20.4 x 22.5 cm
R624.50

ERNEST GEORGE FOSBERY

58. [Surprised man] 1907
charcoal
50.4 x 31.3 cm (image)
53.5 x 34.2 cm (sheet)
R624.3691
Illustrated page 17

MALCOLM FRASER

59. "Shang Chid Mongols - Man and Woman"
for: "Driven Out of Tibet - An Attempt to Pass
From China Through Tibet into India"
in *Century Illustrated Magazine*, April, 1894
oil, crayon and graphite on primed canvas
55.0 x 39.2 cm (image)
55.0 x 40.9 cm (sheet)
R1557

ARTHUR BURDETT FROST

60. "Insurance Agent"
for: "The Trials of Jonathan Goode"
in *Scribner's Magazine*, December, 1920
charcoal and graphite
27.2 x 25.1 cm (image)
36.4 x 29.1 cm (sheet)
R121.5

61. "Circus Day"
Headpiece for: "Circus Day" by Eugene Wood
in *McClure's Magazine*, September, 1905
ink
13.3 x 26.4 cm (image)
23.8 x 36.8 cm (sheet)
R121.1

62. "The End of the Century"
for: *Harper's Weekly*, April, 1896
watercolour and gouache
47.0 x 64.6 cm
R121.6
Illustrated page 112

ERNEST FUHR

63. "Now I guess we understand each other...
This, Pick, is a blank check on my bank
in Yonkers"
for: "The Diamond Jester" by Frank E. Evans
in *Collier's*, October, 1914
watercolour, crayon and gouache
36.1 x 37.8 cm (image)
53.1 x 57.1 cm (sheet)
R624.3122
Illustrated page 34

64. "Lena and Billy swarmed into the room
without waiting for permission, hand in hand,
and smiling happily upon the world. 'Nell, we're
married!' Billy shouted, and then stopped short
at sight of his father-in-law."
for: "Marconi vs. Hymen"
by Frank X. Finnegan
in *Collier's*, September, 1914
charcoal, ink and watercolour
27.7 x 37.7 cm
R624.2444
Illustrated page 39

GEORGE GIBBS

65. "Stephen Decatur attacking the
Tripolitan Captain"
for: "Revenge of Decatur" by George Gibbs
in *Cosmopolitan*, August, 1901
gouache, watercolour and pencil
63.0 x 45.0 cm
R624.1692

JOSEPH J. GOULD

66. " 'Ye can sthay your hand, ould pal,'
says Clivir"
for: "My Life - So Far" by Josiah Flynt
in *Success Magazine*, August, 1907
watercolour and graphite
27.5 x 36.2 cm (image)
29.1 x 37.2 cm (sheet)
R624.3471

GORDON HOPE GRANT

67. "A Bashful Man's Proposal.
The Messenger Boy. Any answer, Lady?"
Cartoon for: *Puck*, February, 1907
watercolour and graphite
46.4 x 37.1 cm
R624.1054

WALTER GRANVILLE-SMITH

68. "The ol' Squire swoh all those witnesses on
the Annual Report of the Postmastah-General"
for: "Strone's Southerner" by Charles Warren
in *Collier's*, June, 1905
watercolour
52.4 x 52.3 cm
R624.1241

ELIZABETH SHIPPEN GREEN [ELLIOTT]

69. "It is a pity you cannot smoke, Michael"
for: "An Incident in the Prefecture of Police"
by Arthur Sherburne Hardy
in *Harper's Monthly Magazine*, 1916
charcoal
30.3 x 37.0 cm (image)
42.5 x 48.3 cm (sheet)
R624.3569
Illustrated page 30

70. "After a number of nights I dared to
touch her hand."
for: "Aurelie" by Arthur Sherburne Hardy
in *Harper's Monthly Magazine*, 1909
watercolour, gouache, charcoal,
crayon and varnish
60.5 x 39.0 cm
R624.4047

DAN SAYRE GROESBECK

71. " 'He's a grand wee lad,' burst
out Hennessy"
for: "Who's Who in Nevada" by Barton Wood
Currie in *Success Magazine*, 1910
watercolour, gouache, ink and graphite
59.8 x 38.7 cm
R624.1386

JAY HAMBIDGE

72. "We deliver that foundling to you as the
representative of the country"
for: "Slaves of Success" by Elliott Flower
in *Collier's Weekly*, September, 1904
graphite
20.9 x 32.7 cm
R624.3437

73. "He waited a moment to make
his shot sure"
for: "The Middle Ground Where Labor and
Capital Failed to Meet" by Edwin Balmer
in *Collier's*, September, 1906
watercolour, ink and graphite
25.5 x 43.3 cm (image)
31.8 x 49.7 cm (sheet)
R624.1127

74. "All hands to rescue a derailed electric
car - A frequent incident of the first traffic
in Richmond."
for: "The Electric Railway"
by Frank J. Sprague
in *Century Illustrated Magazine*, August, 1905;
used again for: "The Story of the Trolley"
in *St. Nicholas Magazine*, September, 1922
gouache
46.5 x 31.0 cm (image)
49.5 x 33.3 cm (sheet)
R624.3626
Illustrated page 13

CHARLOTTE HARDING [BROWN]

75. "The Village About the
Towering Chimneys"
for: "A New Occupation: The Welfare
Manager" by Lillie Hamilton French in
Century Illustrated Magazine, November, 1904
charcoal
62.3 x 36.5 cm
R624.3157
Illustrated page 63

GEORGE MATTHEWS HARDING

76. [Dock in a foreign port]
charcoal
61.6 x 62.7 cm
R624.3744
Illustrated page 116

77. "They Was Women"
Headpiece for: "They Was Women" by
Richard Washburn Child in *Colliers*, June, 1907
charcoal, gouache and varnish
42.8 x 63.2 cm
R624.1626

HERMAN HEYER

78. "Just then there came a knock at the door, and a stranger entered; - an old man weak and ill. He said he was hungry and asked for food. The mother looked at her children and the children's eyes said, 'yes.' Without a word she pointed to the table and bade the stranger eat."
for: "The Shameful Misuse of Wealth"
by Cleveland Moffett
in *Success*, April, 1904
graphite, watercolour, gouache, crayon and ink
36.2 x 38.9 cm
R624.2430

WILLIAM ELY HILL

79. [In a theatre box]
charcoal, gouache, watercolour, ink and graphite
33.2 x 50.7 cm
R624.2411
Illustrated page 59

LUCIUS WOLCOTT HITCHCOCK

80. "She sat in silence watching him. It all seemed so curiously different from what she had expected."
for: "The Amazing Widow" by Anne Warner
in *Collier's*, June, 1915
charcoal, graphite and ink
49.5 x 60.4 cm
R624.3823
Illustrated page 27

ROBERT BRUCE HORSFALL

81. [Seals]
watercolour and gouache
36.2 x 34.6 cm (image)
R624.2200

HENRY HUTT

82. [Woman nursing a wounded soldier]
for: "Metamorphosis of Corfina Delictum,"
July, 1899 (Mexico)
gouache, ink, watercolour and graphite
72.3 x 56.0 cm
R624.3095
Illustrated page 107

WILLIAM LEROY JACOBS

83. "Isabel, I can't find my keys anywhere. I wish you'd just feel in baby's mouth"
Cartoon for: *Life*, December, 1907
ink, charcoal and gouache
52.0 x 43.7 cm (image)
62.7 x 53.0 cm (sheet)
R624.1911

ARTHUR EDWARD JAMESON

84. [Couple in a restaurant]
gouache, watercolour and graphite
61.4 x 39.7 cm
R624.56

MARTIN JUSTICE

85. "He knew that he was making himself agreeable"
for: "Kerrigan's Diplomacy"
by L. Frank Tooker
in *Century Illustrated Magazine*, March, 1905
gouache, ink, charcoal and graphite
36.0 x 38.1 cm (image)
47.7 x 47.3 cm (sheet)
R624.1595

86. "The False Alarm"
Headpiece for: "The False Alarm" by Octavus Roy Cohen in *Collier's*, April, 1915
gouache, watercolour and graphite
23.4 x 53.7 cm
R624.3156

GERTRUDE ALICE KAY

87. [The haircut]
charcoal and gouache
58.8 x 44.3 cm
R624.1889

ARTHUR IGNATIUS KELLER

88. "Songs Mother Taught Me"
Harper and Brothers, 1923
watercolour, charcoal and graphite
38.5 x 54.2 cm
R624.1345

89. [Riot on the steps]
charcoal
57.0 x 76.8 cm
R624.1900

ROLLIN KIRBY

90. "If we all insist, fellow stockholders, I see no way out of it but to fight a duel"
for: "The Rowena O'Toole Company"
by Ellis Parker Butler
in *St. Nicholas Magazine*, January, 1906
gouache, watercolour and graphite
46.7 x 53.6 cm
R624.2928

OTTO LANG

91. "You derned fool! If you do me out of the sale of land..."
for: "Penury Popham" by Anne O'Hagan
in *Success Magazine*, October, 1906
ink and graphite
33.5 x 23.4 cm
R624.3282
Illustrated page 21

GERALD LEAKE

92. " 'Little Merry Smith,' he said, 'you're a wonder!' "
for: "Merry's Case" by Charlotte Sedgwick
in *St. Nicholas Magazine*, August, 1916
oil on canvas
68.6 x 49.2 cm (image)
79.2 x 53.2 cm (sheet)
R624.3754
Illustrated page 76

WILLIAM ROBINSON LEIGH

93. " 'You know it was not, Becky' "
for: "The Red Motor" by Elizabeth New McKeen in *Success Magazine*, November, 1907
crayon, gouache and graphite
63.8 x 44.6 cm
R624.1674

HARRY A. LINNELL

94. [Mother kissing her children good-bye] 1909
watercolour and charcoal
23.3 x 44.5 cm
R624.2414
Illustrated page 72

JOHN NORVAL MARCHAND

95. "The Captain called him to his side and spoke a few encouraging words that did much to quiet the nerves of the plucky quarter-back"
for: " 'Baby Elton,' the Quarter-Back"
by L.W. Quirk in *St. Nicholas Magazine*, November, 1902
gouache, watercolour and graphite
58.0 x 38.5 cm
R624.1245

FRANK BIRD MASTERS

96. [Older and younger women meeting in kitchen]
charcoal, gouache, graphite and watercolour
28.2 x 60.1 cm
R624.1384
Illustrated page 19

97. "If you take my life, it surely
will not help you"
for: "Two Aspirants" by Alvah Milton Kerr
in *Success Magazine*, June, 1907
charcoal, gouache, chalk, watercolour and ink
54.5 x 48.5 cm
R624.3696

HARRY A. MATHES

98. [Two women embracing as man waits
at the door] 1909
charcoal and watercolour
50.6 x 41.8 cm
R624.1247

WALLACE MORGAN

99. "My guardian was looking down at me, and
I was extremely annoyed at having been so
suddenly awakened"
for: "The Dawn Patrol" by Robert A. Anderson
in *McClure's Magazine*, August, 1919
charcoal and crayon
44.9 x 30.5 cm
R624.1863
Illustrated page 105

100. "Over the Top"
charcoal
43.5 x 32.1 cm
R624.1866

PETER SHEAF HERSHEY NEWELL

101. "It is easy to get into conversation. You
drop down beside a newcomer, and say: 'Good
morning. What is the matter with you?'"
for: "Coddling The Ego" by Maude Radford
Warren in *Collier's*, February, 1913
gouache, watercolour, graphite and ink
24.6 x 32.6 cm
R624.4344

FLORENCE ENGLAND NOSWORTHY

102. [Christmas girl]
St. Nicholas Magazine
charcoal, watercolour and graphite
49.3 x 37.4 cm
R624.13

THORNTON OAKLEY

103. "The Colliery Huns returning home
from work"
for: "In the Anthracite Region,"
pictures by Thornton Oakley
in *Century Illustrated Magazine*,
September, 1906
charcoal
86.4 x 59.1 cm
R624.3665
Illustrated page 66

WILLIAM OBERHARDT

104. "The Human Side of Business"
Headpiece for: "The Human Side of Business"
by Arthur Warren in *Success Magazine*,
June, 1908
charcoal and gouache
60.4 x 51.8 cm
R624.4052

ROSE CECIL O'NEILL [LATHAM WILSON]

105. "A Cheerful Loser"
Miss Johnson. - 'He admits dat he gambles - but
he says he only does it to try to git money
'nough for us to git mahried on!'
Miss Jackson. - 'Wal. Ah reckon dat's de tryfe.
Dey say he's jes de cheerfullest loser in
Blacksville.'"
for: *Puck*, 1903
ink
39.0 x 56.3 cm
R624.1132
Illustrated page 22

106. "One method.
Mistress. - 'Now, Bridget when you want to
leave, I shall expect you to give me two weeks
notice!'
Bridget. - 'Oi always do, mum, - and leave juhst
fowe minutes afterward.'"
[cartoon] for: *Puck*, December, 1903
ink, graphite and crayon
36.4 x 52.8 cm
R624.1236
Illustrated page 32

CLARA ELSENE WILLIAMS PECK

107. "The Tournament at Pentecost was
at its height"
charcoal, watercolour, ink and varnish
41.9 x 29.1 cm
R624.484
Illustrated page 14

* 108. "Autumn"
Cover design for: *Collier's*, October, 1908
gouache, watercolour, ink and graphite
59.1 x 40.1 cm
R624.454
Illustrated page 55

HENRY JARVIS PECK

109. "How many of these ladies
have you married?"
for: "The Hermit" by Joseph C. Lincoln
in *Success Magazine*, November, 1907
charcoal
49.3 x 58.2 cm
R624.2513

ERNEST CLIFFORD PEIXOTTO

110. "Canal connecting France and Belgium,
showing tow-paths and shade trees"
for: "Political Problems of Europe"
by Frank A. Vanderlip
in *Scribner's Magazine*, 1905
watercolour and graphite
29.6 x 23.6 cm (image)
41.8 x 30.9 cm (sheet)
R624.1561

GERALD W. PETERS

111. "The Registry Desk, Ellis Island"
for: "In the Gateway of Nations" by Jacob A.
Riis in *Century Illustrated Magazine*, March,
1903;
used again for: "The Hopes of the Hyphenated"
by George Creel in *Century Illustrated
Magazine*, January, 1916
crayon and ink
64.4 x 51.3 cm
R624.2097
Illustrated page 64

HERMAN PFEIFER

*112. [Boys fleeing]
Cover design for: *Circle Magazine*
charcoal, gouache, watercolour and ink
60.2 x 42.7 cm
R624.4006
Illustrated page 54

HENRY CLARENCE PITZ

113. " 'Look,' said Clim of the Clough,
'See you not the King's seal?' "
for: "Bell, Clim of the Clough, William of
Cloudesley" by George Philip Knapp
in *St. Nicholas Magazine*, March, 1921
charcoal and gouache
37.8 x 42.6 cm
R624.2346

HARRY SPAFFORD POTTER

114. "She became aware — with a sudden
mortification, of her over elaborate
appearance."
for: "Running Water" by Alfred Edward
Woodley Mason in *Century Illustrated
Magazine*, August, 1906
gouache, watercolour and graphite
72.1 x 49.0 cm
R624.2343
Illustrated page 60

JAMES MOORE PRESTON

115. "If some wood-chopping clown / should
come from the town..."
for: "Santa Claus' Tree" by Wallace Irwin
in *Success Magazine*, December, 1907
charcoal and watercolour
30.3 x 22.1 cm
R624.3418
Illustrated page 75

MAY (MARY) WILSON
WATKINS PRESTON

116. "There are so many things M could do..."
unpublished drawing for: *Century*
ink and graphite
25.4 x 21.3 cm
R624.2014

117. [Couple on ship's deck] 1902
charcoal and crayon
38.3 x 48.2 cm
R624.3183

NORMAN MILLS PRICE

***118.** Cover design for: *St. Nicholas Magazine*,
September, 1916
gouache, watercolour, ink and graphite
42.1 x 31.8 cm
R624.2823
Illustrated page 41, and front cover

HENRY PATRICK RALEIGH

119. "Clara bowed her head in shame"
for: "Revival at Dedlay" by Bert Leston Taylor
in *Associated Sunday Magazine*, January, 1908
watercolour, charcoal and crayon
44.9 x 42.0 cm
R624.1264

CHARLES M. RELYEA

120. "Catching Razorbills and removing the
Bird from the net"
for: "Bird Rock" by Frank M. Chapman in
Century Illustrated Magazine, July, 1899
gouache and watercolour
30.2 x 41.7 cm
R624.1367

***121.** [Luncheon]
watercolour, crayon, gouache and graphite
62.2 x 39.2 cm (image)
64.0 x 41.0 cm (sheet)
R624.2498
Illustrated page 58

122. "Rip's Return" 1899
watercolour and graphite
42.0 x 23.8 cm
R624.1191

T.G. RICHARDSON

123. [Female diver]
charcoal, watercolour, gouache and crayon
30.8 x 20.8 cm
R624.2030

JACK MANLEY ROSE

124. "Bringing in the Yule Log"
for: *St. Nicholas Magazine*, January, 1911
ink and gouache
22.4 x 50.6 cm
R624.1143

OLIVE RUSH

125. "Preparing the Christmas Plum Pudding"
for: *Success*, December, 1903
charcoal and gouache
50.2 x 36.8 cm
R624.2891

CHARLES NICOLAS SARKA

***126.** "Dutch sat down and fanned himself with
his hat. 'Den we stay here all the summer' "
for: "The Tenderfoot goes Alligator Hunting"
in *Success Magazine*, 1910
watercolour and graphite
37.8 x 49.9 cm
R624.2822
Illustrated pages 52 and 88

OSCAR FREDERICK SCHMIDT

127. "The Band struck bravely into 'America,'
bound to honor their new-found friends"
for: "Two Pioneers" by Eveline Warner
Brainerd in *St. Nicholas Magazine*, May, 1923
charcoal, gouache and ink
69.4 x 63.3 cm
R624.3755

FRANK EARLE SCHOONOVER

128. "He worked with the air of a man who has
come at last to some decision, turned to reach
for the towel - looked into the muzzle of his own
gun, with his daughter's resolute eyes
behind it"
for: "A Clean Shave" by Grace MacGowan
Cooke in *Century Illustrated Magazine*,
November, 1912
oil on canvas
55.3 x 83.8 cm
R624.3083

***129.** "Building the lynx cabane"
for: "Breaking Trail" in *Scribner's Magazine*,
May, 1905
pastel, gouache and charcoal
63.9 x 47.7 cm
59.35.2
Illustrated pages 56 and 95

RAYMOND SISLEY
[HERBERT MORTON STOOPS]

130. [Trenches of World War One]
charcoal and watercolour
37.4 x 49.4 cm
R624.1809
Illustrated page 108

THORNTON DRAKE SKIDMORE

131. "Staring, his mouth open, his hands spread
over the heap of jewels on the table."
for: "The Six Rubies" by Justus Miles Forman
in *Collier's*, December, 1912
charcoal and gouache
31.5 x 26.8 cm
R624.2368

SARAH KATHERINE SMITH

132. "The supper party riding home across
the snow"
for: "The Housekeeping Adventurers of the
Junior Blairs" in *St. Nicholas Magazine*,
February, 1914
charcoal
34.9 x 43.9 cm
R624.1308

FRANK SNAPP

133. " 'He told me he bought it from a rich
woman,' said Pearl, 'And he wanted me to put
it on to see how I looked' "
for: "The Love Affair of No. 9" by Louis
Weadock in *Collier's*, January, 1914
watercolour
42.1 x 58.3 cm
R624.1163

PAUL C. STAHR

134. [Couple fishing] August, 1912
charcoal and watercolour
49.2 x 67.6 cm
R624.2907
Illustrated page 79

ALICE BARBER STEPHENS

135. "While the Grandfather clock ticked ten
times they stared at each other, and then a
wave of deep red poured over his face and his
mouth twitched."
for: "Where Thieves Break In" by Josephine
Daskam Bacon in *Collier's*, May, 1909
charcoal and watercolour
50.5 x 76.0 cm
R624.1858
Illustrated page 91

136. "This is the mother my father gave me long ago"
for: "Ultima's Mothers" by Ethel Watts Mumford Grant in *Success Magazine*, 1908
charcoal and pastel
57.1 x 49.5 cm
R624.3013
Illustrated page 71

WALTER KING STONE

137. "The Wildcat is the shyest animal of our Eastern Forests, and yet the fiercest and most formidable"
for: "Our Wild Animal Neighbors" by Walter Prichard Eaton
in *Harper's Monthly Magazine*, January, 1918
charcoal, watercolour and gouache
54.8 x 35.9 cm
R392.16

THURE de THULSTRUP

138. " 'Sit down,' he said, 'and write.' "
for: "Roden's Corner" by Henry Seton Merriman in *Harper's New Monthly Magazine*, January, 1898
watercolour, gouache and graphite
38.8 x 44.1 cm
R624.1289

MAUD THURSTON

139. "Turkish coffee, made at the table by our hostess concluded the feast"
for: "Dances For Debutantes" by Mrs. Burton Kingsland in *Success Magazine*, January, 1906
pencil and ink
32.1 x 24.2 cm
R624.3490

OTTO TOASPERN

140. "A Whispered Dialogue: The Husband: You are right! It must be Burglars! Where is my revolver? The Wife: Down in the library over the desk. You know I tied ribbons on it for an ornament."
Cover design for: *Life* June, 1895
crayon and ink on textured paper
28.8 x 34.7 cm
R624.3674

GEORGE TIMOTHY TOBIN

141. Cover for: *Century Illustrated Magazine*, June 30, 1903
charcoal, gouache and ink
57.5 x 36.7 cm
R624.4343

STUART TRAVIS

142. [Woman giving calling card to maid] 1901
ink, watercolour, gouache and graphite
55.5 x 37.6 cm
R624.1342

LESLIE HOLLAND TURNER

143. " 'Thanks to the salt, here we are,' said Bill as he stood up on his feet feeling himself of bruises"
watercolour, crayon and graphite
26.9 x 30.0 cm
R624.2418

CHARLOTTE WEBER-DITZLER

144. "Flung him into the other end of the room."
for: "The Late Tenant" by Gordon Holmes in *Associated Sunday Magazine*, September, 1906
charcoal, gouache, crayon and graphite
62.0 x 44.2 cm
R624.1888

IRVING RAMSAY WILES

145. "A Bride of the Desert"
for: "Fez, The Mecca of the Moors" in *Century Illustrated Magazine*, August, 1893
watercolour and graphite
55.3 x 37.2 cm
R624.18
Illustrated page 115

ADA CLENDENIN WILLIAMSON

146. "The little wad of flesh before her became of all things the most desirable"
for: "Janey and the Stork" by Inez Haynes Gillmore in *Success Magazine*, 1910
charcoal and crayon
50.2 x 37.6 cm
R624.85

ALICE BEACH WINTER

147. [Grandmother and baby]
graphite, gouache, ink and shellac
14.1 cm diam.
R624.856
Illustrated page 69

FRANKLIN T. WOOD

148. [Laborers confronting man]
charcoal
60.0 x 40.9 cm
R624.2842

GEORGE HAND WRIGHT

149. " 'Now,' said he, 'you'll have to let me carry you' "
for: "Ma'am" by Groverneur Morris in *Collier's*, September, 1909
charcoal, gouache and watercolour
45.2 x 63.1 cm
R624.1205

150. "Before we would move he had leaped the intervening space and was at the other's throat"
for: "Banjo Nell" by James Hooper in *Collier's*, February, 1910
charcoal, watercolour and gouache
41.8 x 56.8 cm
R624.2476

151. "She covered her eyes, writhing"
for: "The Harvest Moon" by Justus Miles Forman in *Collier's*, January, 1909
watercolour, gouache and charcoal
37.5 x 55.3 cm
R624.2918

FREDERICK COFFAY YOHN

152. [Spanish-American War scene] c.1897-1898
oil on canvas
50.6 x 76.1 cm
R624.2852

ITINERARY

Glenbow Museum, Calgary, Alberta . . . . March 22 - July 13, 1986

Joslyn Art Museum, Omaha, Nebraska . . . . July - August, 1987

High Museum of Art, Atlanta, Georgia . . . . October - November, 1987

Worcester Art Museum, Worcester, Massachusetts . . . . . April - May, 1988

Art Gallery of Ontario, Toronto, Ontario . . . . July - August, 1988

This exhibition has been produced by the
Glenbow Museum, Calgary
with the assistance of the
Canada Council,
Province of Alberta and
City of Calgary.

his volume was published in 1986 by the Glenbow Museum, Calgary, Alberta, to highlight its large collection of American illustrator art. The catalogue is dedicated to Helen Card, an early collector who was largely responsible for gathering the illustrations now at Glenbow. Judy Larson guest-curated the exhibition and was the author of the text. The book was designed by Cathie Faren with production co-ordinated by Rick Budd, photography by Kevin Oke and typesetting by Luana Russell. Printing by Paperworks Press, Calgary, was supervised by Stephen Whitehall; technical advice by Nelson Vigneault. Separations, duotones and halftones were prepared by United Graphic Services, Calgary. The volume was bound by Atlas Book Bindery, Edmonton, Alberta. The text stock is eighty pound Teton, clay and warm white. The cover stock is eighty pound Karma cover, white. The typeface is Century Light. This edition consists of 2,500 copies.